Woman's Day
CROCKERY
CUISINE

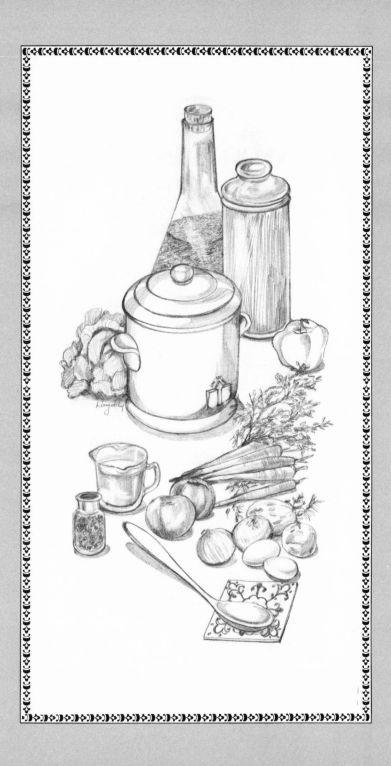

Woman's Day
CROCKERY CUISINE

❧

Slow-Cooking Recipes
for Family and Entertainment

❧

SYLVIA VAUGHN
THOMPSON

Random House New York

Library of Congress Cataloging in Publication Data
Thompson, Sylvia Vaughn Sheekman.
Woman's day crockery cuisine.
Includes index.
1. Electric cookery, Slow. I. Woman's day.
II. Title. III. Title: Crockery cuisine.
TX827.T48   641.5'88   77-6011
ISBN 0-394-41545-0

Manufactured in the United States of America

Illustrations by Lilly Langotsky

2 4 6 8 9 7 5 3

First Edition

For
Glenna McGinnis
with twenty years of love

Acknowledgment

I am grateful to the company of cooks who helped me test endless recipes in order to create the following collection. I am more grateful than I can say to Rheta Resnick for a year and a half of unstinting effort—and to her family and mine for their patience, candor and, finally enthusiasm.

Contents

❦

ONE
WHY AND HOW TO USE THE CROCK

Why Cook in a Crock?	3
Choosing a Crock	3
Equipment Used Inside the Crock	4
Cooking in the Crock	5
Temperature and Time	6

❦

TWO
HOT DRINKS

Non-Alcoholic	11
Chocolate Calda del Rey (Royal Spanish Hot Chocolate)	11
Natasha's Tea	11
Temperance Mull	12
Alcoholic	
Rajah	12
Hot Buttered Rum	13
The Old Gentleman's Coffee	13

❦

THREE
SAUCES

"Sour Cream" for the Crock	17
"Spit-Roasted" Baste for Poultry and Meat	17
Twenty Seasonings Barbecue Sauce	18
Neapolitan Tomato Sauce	18

Cowboy's Slosh   19
Sloppy SuperJoes   19
A Big Batch of Spaghetti Sauce   20
Mushroom Sauce   21
Curry Sauce   22
Double Chocolate Hot Fudge Sauce   23

❦

FOUR
CHEESE AND EGGS

Cooking Cheese and Eggs in the Crock   27
Welsh Rabbit Supper   27
Strata from the Pizzeria   28
Polenta and Cheese Pudding   29
Chili Puff   29
Chili Puff with Chili Sauce   30
Cheese Soufflé   30
Corn Supper Custard   31
School-Night Supper   31

❦

FIVE
DIPS

Making Dips in the Crock   35
Mexican Melted Cheese and Mild Chilies   35
Mexican Macaroni and Cheese   35
Mexican Rabbit   35
Frijoles Cremosos (Creamy Refried Beans)   36
Tostadas Cremosas   36

SIX

SOUPS

All Vegetables	39
Vegetable Soup	39
Lazy Gazpacho	39
Beet Borscht	39
Catalonian Pumpkin Soup	40
Roasted Pumpkin Seeds	40
Leek and Potato Soup	41
French Sorrel Soup	41
Cream of Watercress Soup	41
Creamy Tomato Soup	41
Beans and Legumes	42
Navy Bean Soup	42
Lentil Soup	42
Creamy Split Pea Soup	43
A Little Meat	43
Barley Soup	43
Borshch from Old Russia	44
A Meat Base	45
Onion Soup	45
Turkey Soup Creole	46
Mexican Meatballs in Broth	47
Silky Beef Soup	48
Mixed Meats	
Gumbo	49
Menudo (Mexican Tripe Soup)	50
Barbados Pepper Pot	51
Stocks	51
Triple-Strength Chicken Stock	51
Broth from Bones	52

———— ❧ ————

SEVEN
GROUND MEATS

Cooking Ground Meats in the Crock	57
Casseroles	57
Meat and Vegetables Macedonia	58
Casserole with Artichoke Hearts	58
Cross Creek Casserole	59
Creamy Meat and Macaroni Casserole	60
Layered Enchiladas	61
Rice and Meat	62
Sfogato (Greek Meat and Vegetable Custard)	63
Shepherd's Pie	64
Chili Con Carne	65
Red Flannel Hash	65
Quick Hash and Cabbage	66
Meat Loaves	67
Kitchen Garden Meat Loaf	67
Turkey Loaf with Zucchini	68
Un-stuffed Cabbage	69
Lamb Loaf	70
Meatballs	70
Italian Meatballs	70
Sweet and Sour Meatballs	71
Nippy Meatballs in Mushroom Sauce	72
Meatballs Java with Japanese-style Rice	73
Stuffed Leaves	74
Sweet and Sour Cabbage Rolls	74
Stuffed Grape Leaves	75

❧

EIGHT

BEEF

Cooking Beef in the Crock 79
Braised Beef—Stews 80
  Braised Beef 80
  Beef Stew for a Party 81
  Zrazy (Polish Beef Stew) 82
  Chili Verde (Mexican Beef Stew) 83
  Tahitian Beef Stew 84
  Cholent (Meat and Lima Bean Stew) 85
  Daube Provençale (Beef Stew from
    Provence) 86
  Green Pepper Steak 87
  Flemish Beef in Beer 87
Braised Beef—Stuffed 88
  Stuffed Beef Birds 88
  Mushroom-Stuffed Flank Steak 89
Braised Beef—Bones
  Thai Sweet and Sour Beef Ribs 90
  Short Ribs and Potatoes 91
Crock-Roasted Beef 92
  Pot Roast Paprika 92
  Crock-Roasted Beef 93
  Beef in Cream 93
  A Classic Sauerbraten (German Pot
    Roast) 94
Poached Beef 95
  Basic Boiled Beef 95
  Deviled Corned Brisket of Beef 96
  Irish Corned Beef and Cabbage 96
Roasted Corned Beef 96
  Down-Home Corned Beef 96

NINE

PORK, LAMB AND VEAL

Cooking Pork, Lamb and Veal in the Crock 101
Braised Pork—Stews 103
Crocked Pork and Beans 103
Pork and Limas 103
Mexican Pork and Black Beans 104
Pork and Sauerkraut Stew 104
Braised Pork—Slices 105
Braised Slices of Pork Savoyard 105
Braised Pork—Chops 106
Peppery Pork Chops 106
Spareribs 106
Applesauced Country Ribs 106
Crock-Roasted Pork 107
Succulent Roast Pork with Yams 107
Braised Lamb—Stews 107
Traditional Irish Stew 107
Rumanian Lamb Stew 108
Lamb Shanks Caravanserai 109
Braised Lamb—Roast 110
French Braised Lamb 110
Crock-Roasted Lamb 111
Shoulder of Lamb 111
Crock-Roasted Lamb 111
Poached Lamb 112
Dill-Poached Lamb Dinner 112
Dilled Fresh Pea Soup 112
Braised Veal—Stews 113
Braised Veal in Osso Buco Sauce 113
Gremolata 113
Veal Shank Stew 114
Crock-Roasted Veal 115
Pâté-Stuffed Rolled Breast of Veal 115

Poached Veal   116
   Poached Veal in Creamy Sauce   116

TEN
CHARCUTERIE, VARIETY MEATS AND
MIXED MEATS

Cooking Charcuterie, Variety Meats and   119
   Mixed Meats in the Crock   119
Charcuterie—Pâtés and Terrines   120
   Liver Pâté   120
   Veal and Bacon Terrine   121
Charcuterie—Ham and Sausages   122
   Glazed Ham   122
   Carbonnade of Ham   122
   Carbonnade of Lamb   122
   Sausages in Wine Sauce   123
   Knackwurst in Stout   123
Variety Meats—Braised   124
   Italian Oxtail Stew   124
   Beef and Kidney Ragout   125
   Porkalt   126
   Sweetbreads   127
Variety Meats—Poached   127
   Poached Calves' Liver Tivoli   127
   Tongue à la Diable   128
   Sauce à la Diable   129
Mixed Meats—Baked   129
   Choucroute Garnie   129
   Cassoulet Manqué   130
   Tamale Pie   132
Mixed Meats—Poached   133
   Hochepot (Flemish "Boiled" Dinner)   133

ELEVEN

POULTRY AND A LITTLE GAME

Cooking Poultry and Game in the Crock	137
Braised Chicken and Turkey	138
Basic Chicken or Turkey, Self-Basted	138
Savory Mushroom Turkey	139
Vintner's Chicken	140
Rich Vintner's Chicken	140
Chutney Chicken Legs	141
Orange Curried Chicken Wings	141
Five Flavors Chicken	142
Braised Chicken—Stews	143
Chicken Breasts and Artichoke Hearts	143
Chicken Diana	143
Neapolitan Chicken	144
Venetian Chicken Casserole	145
Polenta	145
Chicken Chanteclair	146
Mexican Chicken with Fruit	147
Arroz con Pollo	148
Crock-Roasted Chicken and Game Birds	149
Roasted Chicken in the Crock	149
Danish Stuffed Chicken	149
Rock Cornish Game Hens or Other Small	149
Game Birds in the Crock	149
Glazed Game Birds	150
Poached Chicken	151
Poulet à la Crème	151
Flemish Chicken Fricassee	152
Coq à la Bière	153
Foil-Wrapped Turkey Fillets	153
Turkey Picnic Rolls	153

Cooked Poultry for Other Purposes   154
Chicken, Turkey and Other Poultry Pre-
   cooked for Casseroles, Sandwiches and
   Other Purposes   154
Cooked or Leftover Poultry   155
   Tetrazzini with Artichoke Hearts   155
   Curry for a Crowd   155
   Curry Garnishes   156
Rabbit   157
   Rabbit, Creole Style   157

❦

TWELVE

FISH

Cooking Fish in the Crock   161
Fresh Fish   162
   Quick Fish Dish   162
   Turbot in Onion Cream   162
   Rolled Fillets of Sole Chablis   163
   Cool Greek Fish with Fresh Mayonnaise   164
      Lemon Broth   165
   Cold Cream Soup from Normandy   166
   Portuguese Fish Stew   167
   Santa Monica Bay Bouillabaisse   167
      Rouille   169
Cooked or Canned Fish   169
   Cheese Custard Fish Supper   169
   Salmon Mousse   170
      Alice Vinegar's Egg Sauce   170
   Italian Sweet-and-Sour Tuna Ragout   171
   Manhattan Clam Chowder   172
Salted Fish   173
   Salt Cod à la Provençale   173

THIRTEEN
PASTAS AND GRAINS

Easy Macaroni and Cheese	177
Chili Macaroni	177
Macaroni and Cheese Pudding	178
Macaroni and Beans, Gardener's Style	179
Lasagne with Eggplant	180
A Perfect Noodle Kugel	180
Green Cheese Cannelloni Casserole	181
Crêpes	182
Tortilla, Bean and Cheese Casserole	183
Chilaquiles de Crema	183
Steamed Rice, White and Brown	184
A Simple Risotto	185
Three-Colored Hat	186
Israeli Barley Supper	187

FOURTEEN
FRESH VEGETABLES

Cooking Fresh Vegetables in the Crock	191
Vegetables Not to Cook in the Crock	192
Asparagus	192
Dried Beans	193
Lentils and Rice	193
Beets	194
Brussels Sprouts	194
Bella's Cabbage, Noodles and Onions	195
Red Red Cabbage	195
Creamy Carrot Shreds	196
Cauliflower	196
Chestnuts	197
Corn on the Cob	197

Eggplant and Rice Supper 197
Rice-Stuffed Green Peppers 198
Sweet Red Peppers 199
Grandma's Okra 199
Sour Creamed Onions 200
Rosemary New Potatoes 200
Potato Slices with Cheese 201
Alsatian Potato Salad 201
Yams and Sweets 202
Quintessential Spinach (and Other Greens) 202
Summer Squashes 203
Zucchini and Tomatoes 203
Acorn Squash Stuffed with an Apple 204
Pumpkin for Pie 204
Anchovied Tomatoes 205
Cool Vegetables, Warm Colors 206

FIFTEEN
FRUITS

Cooking Fruits in the Crock 209
Rosy Applesauce 209
Jellied Apples (or Quinces) 210
Jelly Pears 210
Poires Cardinal (Poached Pears in a Red
    Mantle) 211
Georgena's Peaches 212
Platanos (Mexican Baked Bananas) 212
Pineapple with Rum, Mexican Style 213
Summer Compote 213
Winter Compote 214
    Winter Fool 214
Lizzy's Prunes 215
    Alice's Prunes 215
    Danish Apple Pudding 215

French Apple Pudding 216
Cranberry Sauce 216

❦

SIXTEEN
DESSERTS

Baking Desserts in the Crock 219
Creams 219
Gilded Cream 219
Cheese Dessert 220
Pineapple Cream Cake 221
Pumpkin Cheese 222
Sour Cream Topping 222
Grandma Rose's Pumpkin Custard 223
Sherried Whipped Cream 223
Custards 224
Rich Nut Custard 224
Indian Pudding 224
Puddings 225
Old-Fashioned Tapioca Pudding 225
Rice Pudding 226
Best Bread Pudding Ever 226
Lemon Sauce 227
Lemon Curd Pudding 228
A Chewy, Nutty Graham Pudding 228
Muscat Christmas Pudding 229
Kentucky Hard Sauce 230
Silky Caramel Slices 230
Soufflé 231
Orange Soufflé 231
Marmalade Sauce 231
Chocolate 232
Chocolate Almond Dream 232

SEVENTEEN

CAKES, BREADS AND BREAKFAST CEREALS

"You Baked That . . . in the Crock?!"	235
Cakes	236
Gold Cake—The Basic Crock Cake	236
Victorian Seed Cake	236
Saffron Seed Cake	236
Walnut Cake	237
A Traveling Cake	238
Carrot Cake	239
Cream Cheese Icing	239
Blueberry Crumbles	240
Breads	240
Irish Soda Bread	240
Sweet Poppy Seed Bread	241
Cereals	242
Cooking Cereals in the Crock	242

EIGHTEEN

PRESERVES

The Crock as a Preserving Kettle	245
English Bitter Jelly and Marmalade	245
Springtime Jelly and Jam	247
Peachy Honey	248
Idaho Cherry Conserve	248
Fresh Strawberry Syrup	249
Pumpkin Chutney	250
Summer Mincemeat for Winter Pies	251
Zucchini Relish	251
Spiced Orange Peel	252
French Apple Rings	253
Dog and Badger Chop House Sauce	253

Index	255

One

WHY AND HOW TO USE THE CROCK

WHY COOK IN A CROCK?

We all know the reasons for using a crock:

It stretches time.

It assures controlled cooking, without our having to think about it.

It saves fuel.

It keeps the kitchen cool.

It makes inexpensive cuts of meats succulent and tasty.

It retains vitamins and minerals in the juices.

It's an enormous convenience in special situations, such as a vacation cabin or a boat galley.

It's a cinch to clean.

But when I began cooking in a crock a year and a half ago, I hated it. Everything came out tasting as if it had been "cooked in the crock."

Now I love it because I have the right recipes, designed especially for the crock.

In the following pages you'll find more than 260 tested recipes that will give you the best chicken, the finest creams and custards, delicious vegetables, fish, fruit, cheese and pasta dishes—not to mention casseroles. *None of these recipes would be better cooked in the oven or on top of the stove.* There is an art to cooking in the crock, rewarding art. A time-saving, money-saving, fuel-saving art. And the following recipes should make it possible for you to learn it quickly and effortlessly.

CHOOSING A CROCK

Features to look for in a crockpot include wrap-around heating elements, a removable stoneware interior, a removable cord, a glass top for peeking (the top should never be lifted while cooking, as this slows cooking by as much as a half-hour), an insulated metal exterior, two handles that are easy to grasp, and a click-type High and Low dial. Choose a capacity to suit family needs. If you plan to use a soufflé dish in the cooker, set one into the crock to test for size.

Common sense and the rules for other kitchen electrical equipment apply here. Keep the cord in perfect condition. Set the crock and cord well back on the counter so it can't catch and fall over. Keep the cord away from the heat of the stove. If an extension cord is necessary, make sure it is heavy-duty.

Never set the crock in water. But if the bottom does get wet, shake out all the water and set the crock aside to dry *thoroughly* before using again.

Treat the stoneware as you would any crock—no extremes of temperature at the same time (boiling water poured over something frozen), or it might crack.

EQUIPMENT USED INSIDE THE CROCK

A 5-cup soufflé dish adds enormously to the range of possible dishes. The right-sized soufflé dish is usually referred to as a 6-cup dish, and the number 6 is often embossed on the bottom; its true capacity, however, is about 5⅓ cups.

A sling is a homely invention to use with the soufflé dish. Cut cotton string in 8 lengths about 14 inches long. Knot the pieces together at one end, keeping the other ends separate. Spread this like a little octopus on the counter, set the soufflé dish over it, then use the strings to lift it up and into the crock. Spread ends of string evenly out over the sides of the crock, set on the lid. To lift out, remove the lid and gather up the ends of the strings, lift up and out. A sling will last several months.

A vegetable steamer is available at housewares or health food stores. Buy the aluminum kind with a stem that screws into the center at the top or bottom and sides that fold flat. It is good for stacking stuffed green peppers and such.

Steamer molds are available in 5-cup size, and usually have a tube center. Use one instead of a soufflé dish when appropriate. Buy it in a department store housewares section so that you can first see if it fits into a crock like yours.

Kitchen parchment to be used as a *liner* is available in most department store housewares sections. It's reusable and keeps food from sticking. Substitute buttered or oiled brown shopping bag paper, if you want.

EQUIPMENT USED OUTSIDE THE CROCK

A good sharp knife is crucial to crock cookery. Or a food processor, of course, which is invaluable. A cleaver is very useful for cutting bones to fit them into the crock for soup.

A wok or large heavy skillet makes browning a breeze. Fit it with a glass lid which will keep spattering down and let you see inside.

A large glass measuring pitcher is helpful when making layered dishes.

An electric timer, into which you plug the crock and which is set to go on at a certain hour, and then forget about, is invaluable. With a timer, you don't have to cook chicken all day on Low, for example, when it's better cooked more quickly on High.

Note: Do not leave foods that might spoil in the crock without any heat for too long a time. Use your own judgment depending on the outside temperature and the kind of food you will cook. However, more than two hours in hot weather is unwise for any food.

COOKING IN THE CROCK

Seasoning is the critical success-or-failure element in crock cooking. Add salt and pepper at the beginning, not at the end. Use seasonings with verve: lemon juice, browned onions, garlic, dry vermouth, lots of freshly ground pepper, chopped parsley, and good herbs. Use dried whole leaf herbs: fresh and ground herbs tend to lose flavor in the crock.

Browning is always a good idea. It cuts down on cooking time and adds flavor and much-needed color. When browning, use high heat and stir almost constantly.

Liquid required for crock cooking should, as a general rule, be one-third less than in conventional recipes. The crock pulls juice from everything! Since the crock will not reduce liquids, conventional sauces will thin out in the crock and need the support of cottage cheese or creamed soups.

Quantities will vary, but the crock should never be less than one-quarter full. Unless covered with liquid, hard-to-cook things like vegetables don't cook successfully in the upper quarter of the crock. If the crock is full, it is often wise to take things out of the crock halfway through the cooking period and reverse the order, top to bottom, for even cooking.

Removing awkward foods, like meat loaf, will be easier if you line the crock first with kitchen parchment or buttered brown paper.

Draining crock juices must be done with care. It is best to remove the contents of the crock, pour off the juices and then return food to the crock.

Tasting for seasoning, just before serving, is always important.

"Servings" are modest portions; do not confuse servings with the number of people to be served.

Keeping foods hot is not a function of the crock. Although many foods will hold on Low for 1 or 2 hours without losing quality, those with thickened sauces or gravies will begin to thin out after an hour or so.

Adapt your crock if it doesn't follow the description on page 3. Follow a few of these recipes, cooking the dish until done. Make a note of the time, calculate the difference in timing and make that change with each of these recipes. Some recipes will not work with crocks that heat from the bottom. Check the instructions in your booklet.

TEMPERATURE AND TIME
Crock Temperatures upon Which These Recipes Were Based

TIME	LOW	HIGH
½ hour	108°	150°
¾ hour	124°	168°

TIME	LOW	HIGH
1 hour	135°	183°
1½ hours	154°	250°
2 hours	168°	283°
2½ hours	183°	300°
3 hours	200°	315°
3½ hours	208°	319°
4 hours	212°	330°
5 hours	212°	333°
6 hours	212°	335°
7 hours	212°	340°
8 hours	212°	340°

2 hours on Low generally equals 1 hour on High. If a recipe calls for 8 hours on Low, you can cook it on High part of the time either at the beginning or the end. If you have to serve dinner sooner than expected, you can switch from Low to High and cook for half the remaining time. But don't cook food covered with liquid on High once the temperature hits 212° or it will be boiled.

Keeping track of time can be done with a white grease pencil from a stationer's. Mark down on the lid the time you began the cooking.

Cooking in advance, when feasible, is indicated by an asterisk (*). You can prepare a dish up to that point and refrigerate it overnight if desired. In addition, almost any soup, stew or braised dish is better reheated the day after cooking.

Reheating in the crock to a temperature of 185° to 190° requires about 2½ hours on Low or 1 hour on High. When putting chilled food in the crock, add about 15 minutes to Low or 8 to 10 minutes to High.

Altitude cooking requires increasing the cooking time 1 hour on Low or ½ hour on High for every 1,000 feet above 4,000 feet.

Two

HOT DRINKS

CHOCOLATE CALDA DEL RAY
(ROYAL SPANISH HOT CHOCOLATE)

Use a vegetable peeler to cut the orange peel in a long spiral.

8 ounces chocolate (sweet
  for children, semi-sweet
  for adults)
3 cups half-and-half or
  cream
2 cups milk
1 cup strong coffee
2 tablespoons brown sugar

1 teaspoon vanilla
1 teaspoon cinnamon
½ teaspoon allspice
½ teaspoon nutmeg
Tiny pinch of salt
Peel of 1 orange
½ pint whipping cream

Set crock at High. Break in chocolate, add half-and-half, milk, coffee, brown sugar, vanilla, spices and salt. Stir and cover. Cook, stirring thoroughly every 15 minutes, until chocolate has melted completely, about 1 hour. Add orange peel and stir. Serve immediately, or turn crock to Low and keep covered, removing orange peel after 15 or 20 minutes. Whip the cream. Stir well, then ladle the chocolate into cups and dollop with the cream. *Makes 8–9 servings.*

NATASHA'S TEA

For each cup you'll serve:
½ teaspoon Earl Grey tea
1 teaspoon red cherry or
  strawberry preserves

5 ounces boiling water
1 thin slice lemon

Place tea and preserves in crock. Pour boiling water over them. Cover, heat 1 hour on High or 2½ hours on Low. Add lemon slices. Ladle into cups.

You can strain the tea and hold it another hour on Low.

❦

TEMPERANCE MULL

2 cups cranberry juice
   cocktail
2 cups apple cider
¼ cup brown sugar or to
   taste

8 whole cardamom pods
4 cinnamon sticks
6 cloves
6 thin orange slices

Blend juices, brown sugar, cardamom and cinnamon in crock. Cover and steep overnight. Cook 1 hour on High or 2½ hours on Low. Stick 1 clove in each orange slice and add to crock 10 minutes before serving. Serve in punch cups, each garnished with an orange slice. *Makes 6–7 servings.*

❦

RAJAH

This mull may be prepared a day or two in advance, refrigerated and then reheated. It is very useful for entertaining. The recipe may be doubled.

3 oranges
1¾ cups sugar

1 fifth claret

Roast oranges in 350° oven for 25 minutes. Set in crock. Add sugar and half the bottle of claret. Cover and let steep overnight. Cook 1 hour on High or 2 hours on Low. With heat on remove oranges and squeeze out juice. Strain juice into crock, add remaining wine and stir to blend. Cover and cook 1 to 2 hours more. Serve in punch cups. *Makes 8–10 servings.*

HOT BUTTERED RUM

1½ cups dark Jamaica rum
3 tablespoons butter
¾ teaspoon ground cloves
¾ teaspoon ground allspice

3 tablespoons powdered
sugar
2½–3 cups boiling water,
according to taste

Mix all ingredients in crock. Cover, cook 1 hour on High or 2½ hours on Low. Stir well before ladling into mugs. *Makes 6 servings.*

THE OLD GENTLEMAN'S COFFEE

6 cups very strong coffee
⅓ cup brown sugar
8 2-inch strips orange peel
32 whole cloves

16 whole allspice or
coriander berries
8 cinnamon sticks
¾ cup cognac or brandy

Blend all but the cognac or brandy in crock. Cover, cook 1 hour on High or 2½ hours on Low. Carefully warm ¼ cup cognac in ladle over a burner; do not let it catch fire. Hold over crock and set ablaze with match. Pour into crock, lifting coffee with ladle over and over to keep flame alive. When flame is out, add remaining brandy. Serve, ladling 1 strip peel, a few spices and 1 stick cinnamon into each cup. *Makes 8 servings.*

Three

SAUCES

"SOUR CREAM"
FOR THE CROCK

Substitute this for sour cream in long-cooking casseroles. It won't thin out or break down as dairy sour cream might.

1 cup (8 ounces) cottage or cream cheese

1 can condensed cream of onion, mushroom, chicken

or other suitably flavored soup

1–2 tablespoons lemon juice

Blend ingredients until smooth in blender, food processor or mixer. *Makes 2¼ cups.*

"SPIT-ROASTED" BASTE
FOR POULTRY AND MEAT

This makes unbrowned poultry and meat look and taste as though it came from a barbecue pit.

2 tablespoons catsup

1 teaspoon bottled gravy coloring

1 teaspoon Worcestershire sauce

2 drops liquid smoke

Blend together and brush on meat or poultry. Cook according to basic recipe. *Enough for about 3 pounds poultry or meat.*

TWENTY SEASONINGS BARBECUE SAUCE

This will keep indefinitely in the refrigerator.

1 large onion, chopped fine
3 cloves garlic, chopped fine
1 12-ounce can tomato paste
1 cup mild enchilada sauce
1 cup apple butter
1 cup dark corn syrup
1 cup dark brown sugar
¾ cup strong coffee
½ cup Worcestershire sauce
½ cup beef bouillon
  powder
¼ cup prepared mustard

2 tablespoons bottled gravy
  coloring
2 teaspoons liquid smoke
½ teaspoon Tabasco sauce
2 1¼-ounce packets beef
  and mushroom soup mix
1 teaspoon paprika
½ teaspoon allspice
½ teaspoon thyme
½ teaspoon oregano
½ bay leaf

Mix all ingredients in crock. Cover and cook 9 hours on Low, stirring once or twice. *Makes 7 cups.*

NEAPOLITAN TOMATO SAUCE

Slow-simmered in a heavy skillet, this sauce cooks down thick and the oil floats to the top. Slow-simmered in the crock, the sauce remains thin and does not reduce in volume, but the flavor is remarkably deep and the oil is sleekly blended in. No salt or pepper is necessary.

1 cup olive oil
2 28-ounce cans Italian-style
  tomatoes

Cooked pasta
Freshly grated Parmesan
  cheese

Pour oil into crock. Remove tomatoes from cans with slotted spoon, put in crock, break up and stir. Cover, cook

14 hours on Low, turn to High and cook 1 hour more. Turn into blender or food processor and process just enough to blend; there should be nuggets of tomato in sauce. Serve with pasta and freshly grated Parmesan cheese. *Makes 6 cups.*

❦

COWBOY'S SLOSH

If you have a basic sauce on hand and keep thin sheets of ground meat in the freezer ready to be crumbled into the crock, you can prepare this dinner in an hour. Add canned, drained kidney or pinto beans to stretch this a bit.

1 pound lean ground beef, veal, turkey or sausage	*About 1¾ cups Twenty Seasonings Barbecue Sauce (p. 18)* *Hot cornbread*

Set crock at High. Crumble in uncooked lean meat. (If meat is fatty, brown it separately, drain and add to crock.) Stir in sauce. Cover and cook 1 hour, stirring once. Ladle over hot split cornbread. *Makes 5–6 servings.*

❦

SLOPPY SUPERJOES

1 packet soy protein extender, equivalent to 8 ounces ground meat	*1 cup thick catsup*
1 onion, chopped	*1 teaspoon Worcestershire sauce*
1 clove garlic, minced	*¼ teaspoon salt*
2 tablespoons oil	*¼ teaspoon lemon juice*
1 pound lean ground beef	*Hot cooked noodles or macaroni or buns or pita bread or turkey*
1 12-ounce can corn	
1 8-ounce can tomato sauce	

Soak soy extender in water according to package directions. Brown onion and garlic lightly in oil. Crumble meat into pan, brown lightly, then mix in corn, tomato sauce, catsup, Worcestershire sauce, salt and lemon juice. Turn into crock. Cover, and cook 3½ hours on Low or 1 hour on High, stirring once. Skim off fat. Stir, then ladle over split buns, into pita, or over noodles, macaroni or turkey. *Makes 8 servings.*

———————— 🌱 ————————

A BIG BATCH OF SPAGHETTI SAUCE

2 16-ounce cans tomatoes
1 29-ounce can tomato purée
1 4-ounce can mushroom
    pieces and stems
4 carrots, shredded
3 large onions, chopped fine
1 green pepper, chopped
    fine
1 stalk celery, chopped fine
3 cloves garlic, minced
¼ cup olive oil
1½ pounds lean ground
    beef

½ cup dry red wine
½ cup chopped parsley
1 tablespoon beef bouillon
    powder
1 teaspoon sweet basil
½ teaspoon thyme
1 bay leaf
¼ teaspoon freshly ground
    pepper or to taste
1 teaspoon salt

Empty canned tomatoes, tomato purée and mushrooms into crock, breaking up tomatoes. Sauté the carrots, onions, green pepper, celery and garlic in oil in a large heavy skillet, cooking until soft. Crumble in meat and continue sautéeing until meat has browned but is still slightly pink. Turn into crock. Deglaze skillet with wine and add to crock together with the remaining ingredients. Stir thoroughly, cover and set crock in large pan to catch overflow. Cook 1 hour on High, stir, then cook 2½ hours more, stirring occasionally. Add more salt and pepper to taste. *Makes about 3 quarts, enough for 3 pounds pasta, about 12 servings.*

MUSHROOM SAUCE

This sauce is good with absolutely anything. Try it with chunks of leftover turkey, canned tuna, steamed broccoli or hard-cooked eggs.

2 cups cottage cheese
1 10¾-ounce can condensed cream of mushroom soup
8 to 12 ounces fresh mushrooms, quartered
6 tablespoons butter or margarine
¼ cup flour
¾ cup half-and-half or cream
½ cup dry white wine

6 tablespoons grated Parmesan cheese
⅛ teaspoon onion powder
⅛ teaspoon white pepper
4 cups 1-inch chunks cooked meat, poultry, seafood, vegetables or hard-cooked eggs or a combination of several of these
½ cup walnuts (optional)
Chopped parsley
Hot cooked noodles or rice

Set crock at High. Smooth cottage cheese in blender, food processor, or put through sieve. Blend in soup. Turn into crock. Brown mushrooms lightly in 4 tablespoons of margarine. Add to crock. In same skillet, melt 2 tablespoons margarine, blend in flour and half-and-half. Whisk in wine, Parmesan, onion powder and pepper. Add to crock and blend thoroughly. Fold in chunks and nuts, if used. Cover, turn to Low and cook for about 2¼ hours, or until hot. Stir once or twice. Sauce will hold up to 3 hours. Serve over noodles or rice and garnish with parsley. *Makes 8–9 servings.*

❧

CURRY SAUCE

Use this simple, basic sauce with meat or poultry, or try it with meatballs, chunks of vegetables, shellfish, fish, leftovers, tuna, or hard-cooked eggs.

3 large onions, chopped
6 cloves garlic, minced
2 tart apples, peeled and
  chopped
¼ cup oil
3½ tablespoons curry
  powder or to taste
2 pounds beef, lamb, pork,
  or poultry cut into 1-inch
  cubes

1 16-ounce can stewed
  tomatoes, drained and
  broken up
1 teaspoon salt or to taste
2 tablespoons cornstarch or
  as needed
¼ cup plain yogurt
Hot cooked rice
Curry Garnishes (p. 156)

Lightly brown onions, garlic and apples in oil. Add curry powder and sauté until blended. Add meat or poultry and sauté until thoroughly coated. Add tomatoes and salt. Turn into crock. Cover, cook on Low from 5 to 6½ hours, until poultry or meat is tender.

Taste for seasoning, adding a little more curry powder if necessary.* (Cover and refrigerate up to 3 days, if desired; reheat in a large heat-proof casserole.) Blend cornstarch and yogurt. Stir into sauce until thickened. Ladle over hot, cooked rice and garnish with curry accompaniments. *Makes 6 servings.*

—— ❦ ——

DOUBLE CHOCOLATE HOT FUDGE SAUCE

This thick sauce will harden over ice cream. Well-wrapped in the refrigerator, it will keep almost indefinitely.

6 ounces milk chocolate
4 ounces unsweetened
chocolate
1 pound caramels

½ cup undiluted evaporated
milk
½ cup strong coffee
1 teaspoon vanilla

Break chocolate into crock. Add the caramels, milk and coffee. Cover and cook 45 minutes on High, or until melted, watching carefully so mixture doesn't burn. Add vanilla and stir to blend thoroughly. *Makes about 3 cups.*

Four

❧

CHEESE AND EGGS

COOKING CHEESE AND EGGS
IN THE CROCK

Cheese dishes and egg dishes are very successfully made in the crock. They can be counted on to finish at the times indicated below.

Preparation	Setting/Time
To melt cheese	HIGH: 20 minutes
To heat cheese and egg blends	HIGH: 45 minutes
To heat large quantities of cheese and egg blends	HIGH: 1¼ hours
Cheese and egg stratas	HIGH: 2½ hours
Soufflés, mousses	HIGH: 1 hour
Egg "puffs" with flour and vegetables	HIGH: 2½ hours
Custards, soft center for sauce	HIGH: 1¼ hours
Custards, firm near center	HIGH: 1¾ hours
Thick dips	LOW: 2 hours; HIGH: 1 hour

WELSH RABBIT SUPPER

3 eggs
6 ounces beer
1½ tablespoons ground
   mustard
5 cups (1¼ pounds)
   shredded cheddar or
   American cheese

¼ cup softened butter or
   margarine
Pinch of salt
5 English muffins

Set crock at High. Blend eggs, beer and mustard together in a bowl. Mix in cheese, margarine and salt. Split and lightly toast muffins. Cut in half crosswise to make half-moons. Butter crock, then make a layer of 5 muffin pieces and top with ¾ cup cheese, repeating 3 times. Spread remaining cheese over top and cover.* Cook 45 minutes or until melted and hot. Serve from crock. *Makes 6 servings.*

VARIATION: Sprinkle cheese layers with any or several of the following: chopped tomatoes, crisp crumbled bacon, sliced or chopped black olives, chopped scallions, lightly browned onions, chopped mild green chiles, chopped ham.

❦

STRATA FROM THE PIZZERIA

Serve this with a salad and fresh fruit for dessert.

1 16-ounce can tomatoes, drained and squeezed dry
1 packet onion-mushroom soup mix
2 tablespoons dried sweet peppers
5½ onion rolls
¼ cup softened margarine

2 2¼-ounce cans sliced black olives, drained
2 cups (8 ounces) shredded jack or other mild cheese
3 cups milk
5 eggs
1 teaspoon basil
¼ teaspoon freshly ground pepper

Purée tomatoes in blender or food processor. Stir with soup mix and sweet peppers to make a paste. Split rolls, then cut in half crosswise to make half-moons. Spread with margarine. Divide paste among roll pieces, spreading it to cover. Butter crock, make a layer of 4 roll pieces, tomato side up. Sprinkle rolls with one-fifth of the olives, then with ⅓ cup cheese; repeat 4 more times using 5 roll piecs in the last 2 layers. Whisk milk, eggs, basil and pepper together. Pour evenly over crock, and top with remaining cheese. Cover and refrigerate 4 to 12 hours. Bake 2½ hours on High. Serve from crock. *Makes 8 servings.*

❦

POLENTA AND CHEESE PUDDING

3 cups cornmeal
7½ cups water
1½ teaspoons salt
2 cups (8 ounces) thinly
sliced imported Fontina
or Swiss cheese

Freshly ground pepper to
taste
Butter
Marinara or spaghetti meat
sauce (optional)

Set crock on High. Slowly whisk cornmeal and salt into 1 quart of boiling water in crock. When smooth, cover. Cook 3 hours undisturbed. Rinse a bowl with cold water, turn in polenta. When cold, turn out and cut into ¼-inch slices. Butter crock. Layer polenta and cheese, beginning and ending with polenta and seasoning with pepper as you go. Dot generously with butter and cover.* Bake 1¼ hours on High, or until hot. Serve from crock with or without sauce. *Makes 6–8 servings.*

❦

CHILI PUFF

6 eggs
1 cup cottage cheese
¼ cup melted margarine
⅓ cup flour
½ teaspoon baking
powder
½ teaspoon oregano
¼ teaspoon salt

1 small onion, finely
chopped
1 clove garlic, minced
1 12-ounce can corn,
drained
1 4-ounce can diced mild
green chilies, drained
2 cups (8 ounces) shredded
mild cheese

Butter crock and set at High 20 minutes before beginning. Beat eggs with mixer until light. Blend in cottage cheese, margarine, flour, baking powder, oregano and salt. Stir in onion, garlic, corn, chilies and cheese. Turn into crock. Lay terry towel over top. Cover and bake 2½ hours. Serve from crock. *Makes 6–8 servings.*

For CHILI PUFF WITH CHILI SAUCE, heat the following ingredients together in a saucepan and ladle over Chili Puff: ½ cup tomato paste; ¾ cup beef broth or water; ½ teaspoon oregano; ⅛ teaspoon garlic powder; 1 15-ounce can chili without beans. *Makes about 3¼ cups, or 10 servings.*

❦

CHEESE SOUFFLÉ

The ingredients differ from a conventional recipe, but the finished soufflé is the same—and a thrill to lift from the crock.

3 eggs, separated	*Salt to taste*
1 6-ounce can cheese sauce	*Freshly ground pepper*
⅔ cup cottage cheese	*Dash of nutmeg or sprin-*
1 heaping cup shredded	*kling of appropriate herb*
mild cheese or chopped,	*1 egg white*
cooked meat, fowl, fish or	*Grated Parmesan cheese*
vegetable	*(optional)*

Set crock at High 20 minutes before beginning. Butter 5-cup soufflé dish. Set over sling (see p. 4). In blender or food processor blend egg yolks with cheese sauce and cottage cheese. Stir in filling. Add seasonings. Add extra egg white to separated whites in small bowl. Beat until stiff but not dry. Fold ⅓ whites into cheese mixture thoroughly, then quickly fold in remaining whites. Turn into soufflé dish. Sprinkle Parmesan on top, if appropriate, then run the width of a spatula blade around edge of dish to make a hat in center. Set in crock, lay terry towel over it. Cover and bake 1 hour. Serve at once. *Makes 4 servings.*

❧

CORN SUPPER CUSTARD

¼ cup melted butter or margarine	1 17-ounce can cream-style corn
¼ cup flour	4 eggs
2 tablespoons grated Parmesan cheese	⅔ cup undiluted evaporated milk
	Chopped parsley

Set crock at High 20 minutes before beginning. Butter 5-cup soufflé dish, dust with a little Parmesan cheese and set over sling (see p. 4). Beat margarine, flour, cheese, corn, eggs and milk until blended. Turn into dish and dust top with more Parmesan. Set in crock. Lay terry towel over it. Cover and bake 1¼ hours (center will be soft and may be used as sauce) or bake ½ hour longer until almost set. Serve from dish, dusted with parsley. *Makes 6–8 servings.*

VARIATION: Add 1 cup lightly browned chopped onion and green pepper.

❧

SCHOOL-NIGHT SUPPER

⅔ cup quick cooking cornmeal or farina	1 cup pitted black olives or 1 4-ounce can chopped mild green chilies or to taste
1 cup cold water	
1 cup boiling water	
1 teaspoon beef or chicken bouillon powder	3 eggs
½ teaspoon salt	¾ cup evaporated milk
1 12-ounce can corn kernels or Mexican-style corn, drained	1 or 2 tablespoons mild taco sauce (optional)
	1 tablespoon onion powder
1⅔ cups shredded cheddar or other mild cheese	½ teaspoon oregano, marjoram or basil
	Paprika

Set crock at High before you begin. Butter 5-cup soufflé dish and set over sling (see p. 4). In small saucepan, stir cold water into cereal. Whisk boiling water into it, then add bouillon powder and salt. Cook over low heat, stirring occasionally, while assembling remaining ingredients: turn corn into soufflé dish, top with 1 cup shredded cheese and drained olives or chilies; beat eggs, milk, taco sauce and onion powder together and pour over dish. Spread cooked cereal on top with fork. Sprinkle with herbs and remaining cheese to cover. Set in crock, cover and cook 1¾ hours. Lift dish out, dust with paprika and serve. *Makes 6 servings.*

Five

※

DIPS

❦

MAKING DIPS IN THE CROCK

The crock is fine for making party dips.

It is too large, too narrow and too tall, however, to make a good fondue pot and should not be used in situations where everyone is dipping at once.

❦

MEXICAN MELTED CHEESE AND
MILD CHILIES

The crock melts cheese without danger of burning it.

1 16-ounce can tomatoes, cored, squeezed dry and chopped
1 4-ounce can chopped mild green chilies, drained and seeded
2 cloves garlic, minced

8 cups (2 pounds) shredded American or cheddar cheese
¼ cup finely chopped onion
¼ cup mild taco sauce or to taste
French bread or tortillas

Toss all ingredients together in crock and cover.* Cook on High until cheese melts, stirring frequently, about 20 minutes. Turn to Low, cook another 1¼ hours or until hot. Serve from crock, dipping with cubes of French bread or quarters of hot buttered tortillas.

For MEXICAN MACARONI AND CHEESE stir this sauce into hot macaroni. *Makes 4–6 servings.*

For MEXICAN RABBIT, ladle sauce over toasted French bread or hot English muffins.

FRIJOLES CREMOSOS
(CREAMY REFRIED BEANS)

1 clove garlic, minced
*2 30-ounce cans refried
   beans*
*1 8-ounce package softened
   cream cheese*
*6 tablespoons mild taco
   sauce or to taste*

2 teaspoons chili powder
*2 teaspoons beef bouillon
   powder*
*½ teaspoon ground cumin
   seed*
Corn chips or tortillas

In mixer blend all ingredients together until smooth. Turn into crock and cover.* Cook 2 hours on Low or 1 hour on High until hot, stirring occasionally. Serve from crock on Low, using corn chips or hot quartered tortillas for dipping. *Makes 1½ quarts.*

For TOSTADAS CREMOSAS, ladle over crisp-fried tortillas, then heap with chopped scallions, chopped tomatoes, and shredded cheese. Add slivers of avocado, cooked chicken or turkey, sliced radishes or other garnishes, if you wish.

Six

❧

SOUPS

❧

VEGETABLE SOUP

8 large fresh tomatoes
1 small carrot, finely chopped
1 small stalk celery with
  leaves, finely chopped
2 whole scallions, finely
  chopped
1 large clove garlic, minced
½ cup chopped parsley
¼ cup chopped green
  pepper

1 tablespoon lemon juice
1 tablespoon salt
¼ teaspoon freshly ground
  pepper
4 cups water
1 cup dry white wine
Grated Parmesan cheese
  (optional)

Dip tomatoes in boiling water about 1 minute, then drop into cold water. Slip off skins and save them. Coarsely chop tomatoes. Put tomatoes and all remaining ingredients except Parmesan into crock and stir to blend. Tie tomato skins in cheesecloth and bury in crock. Cover and cook about 8 hours on Low; the vegetables should still be slightly crisp. Remove cheesecloth. Taste for seasoning. Serve with cheese, if desired. *Makes 10 servings.*

For a LAZY GAZPACHO, serve this soup chilled, adding some finely chopped raw zucchini and cucumber. Float a cube of ice in each bowl, and pass chopped hard-cooked egg to sprinkle over.

❧

BEET BORSCHT

Finely chopped beet greens may be added to the crock with the beets.

8 good-sized beets, peeled
   and shredded
1 onion, peeled and
   shredded
¼ cup white vinegar
2 tablespoons brown sugar

2 tablespoons lemon juice
2 teaspoons dill
1½ teaspoons salt
Sour cream or plain yogurt

Mix beets and onion in crock with vinegar, brown sugar, lemon juice, dill, salt and enough water to come to 1 inch of the top. Cover and cook 10 hours on Low or 5 hours on High, or until beets are tender, stirring once or twice. Taste for seasoning. Serve hot or cold dolloped with sour cream or yogurt. *Makes about 12 servings.*

CATALONIAN PUMPKIN SOUP

3 pounds pumpkin or other
   winter or summer squash
3 whole scallions, finely
   chopped
3 cloves garlic, minced
4 cups chicken broth

1 teaspoon freshly ground
   pepper
1 teaspoon salt
½ teaspoon lemon juice
¼ cup chopped cilantro or
   parsley

Peel pumpkin and scrape off seeds and strings. Cut in 1-inch dice. Mix in crock with scallions, garlic, chicken broth, pepper, salt and lemon juice. Cover and cook 5½ hours on Low, or until tender. Purée soup, adding cilantro or parsley. *Makes 8–10 servings.*

For ROASTED PUMPKIN SEEDS, a bonus for making this soup, rinse seeds free of strings, spread on baking sheet, drizzle with oil, and sprinkle with salt and garlic powder. Roast at 350° until golden, shaking pan once or twice.

❦

LEEK AND POTATO SOUP

*4 medium-sized leeks,
  tender greens included
¼ cup butter or margarine
6 medium-large potatoes
1½ teaspoons salt*

*White pepper to taste
8 cups water or chicken
  broth
½–1 cup cream
  (optional)*

Slice leeks lengthwise, rinse well and slice thin. Sauté in butter until wilted. Peel and thinly slice potatoes. Add to skillet and sauté until coated with butter. Turn vegetables into crock, mix in salt, pepper and water or broth. Cover, cook on Low about 8 hours, or until tender. Purée soup, taste for seasoning. To make it richer, heat cream and swirl in just before serving. *Makes 10 servings.*

For FRENCH SORREL SOUP, use 3 dozen sorrel leaves for 4 cups Leek and Potato Soup. Sauté the sorrel in 1½ tablespoons butter until wilted. Add to crock for last 2 hours of cooking, or reheat soup with sorrel on High for 1 hour. *Makes 4–6 servings.*

For CREAM OF WATERCRESS SOUP, use 2 bunches watercress leaves instead of the sorrel. Serve hot or cold.

❦

CREAMY TOMATO SOUP

*2 medium potatoes, peeled
  and shredded
1 onion, peeled and
  shredded
3 tablespoons oil
3 tablespoons butter or
  margarine
4 large tomatoes, peeled and
  chopped
1 tablespoon lemon juice*

*1½ teaspoons salt
¼ teaspoon white pepper
Pinch of sugar
¼ teaspoon basil
⅛ teaspoon mint
3 cups water
1 tablespoon flour
1 cup milk
Chopped parsley*

In large skillet, sauté potatoes and onion in oil and 2 tablespoons butter until onions are golden. Add tomatoes to skillet and sauté 5 minutes longer. Turn into crock. Mix in lemon juice, salt, pepper, sugar, basil, mint and water. Cover and cook about 4 hours on Low, or until vegetables are tender. Purée soup. Rub remaining tablespoon softened butter and flour together, blend into soup. Add milk and whisk gently to blend. Taste for seasoning and reheat in crock or saucepan. Serve garnished with parsley. *Makes 6–8 servings.*

NAVY BEAN SOUP

1 pound small white beans
8 cups water
1 onion, grated
1 large fresh tomato, peeled and chopped
1 whole scallion, finely chopped
2 cloves garlic, minced

1 pound ham, in 1 piece (optional)
½ cup chopped parsley
1 teaspoon basil
2 teaspoons salt
½ teaspoon freshly ground pepper or to taste

Soak beans overnight in water. Next day, turn all ingredients into crock. Cover and cook 12 hours on Low. Taste for seasoning. Break ham into chunks. *Makes 8 servings.*

LENTIL SOUP

1 cup lentils
3 cups water
1 16-ounce can tomatoes
½ onion, finely chopped
1 small stalk celery with leaves, finely chopped
1 small carrot, finely chopped

¼ green pepper, finely chopped
2 thin slices unpeeled lemon
1 bay leaf
½ teaspoon salt or to taste
Freshly ground pepper to taste

Soak lentils in water overnight. Next day, break up tomatoes and add with juice to crock. Add lentils, soaking water and all remaining ingredients. Cover and cook on Low 12 hours. Taste for seasoning. *Makes 6–8 servings.*

❦

CREAMY SPLIT PEA SOUP

1⅔ cups green or yellow
* split peas*
6 cups water
½ cup sour cream
¼ cup milk
1¾ teaspoons salt
½ teaspoon dill
⅛ teaspoon white pepper
Pinch of ground allspice

Pinch of ground coriander
* (optional)*
2 tablespoons instant flour
* or to taste*
2 tablespoons butter or
* margarine*

Combine split peas and water in crock. Cover and cook on High 3½ hours or until soft. Purée in blender or through food mill and return to crock. Whisk in all remaining ingredients except butter. When thickened, taste for seasoning, then add butter in little knobs. *Makes 6–8 servings.*

❦

BARLEY SOUP

¾ cup pearl barley
8 ounces lean ground beef
* or lamb, or ground turkey*
1 28-ounce can tomatoes
1 clove garlic, minced
4 medium-sized dried
* mushrooms, cut in bits*
1 packet dried onion soup
* mix*

½ cup chopped parsley
½ bay leaf
½ teaspoon freshly ground
* pepper*
½ teaspoon thyme
Plain yogurt, sour cream or
* grated Parmesan cheese*

Place barley in crock. Crumble in meat. Break up tomatoes and add with juice. Fill tomato can with water and add. Add garlic, mushrooms, soup mix, parsley, bay leaf, pepper and thyme. Cover and cook 8 hours on Low or until barley is tender. Taste for seasoning. Serve with yogurt, sour cream or Parmesan cheese. *Makes 6–8 servings.*

❦

BORSHCH FROM OLD RUSSIA

12 ounces beef neck, shin,
    shanks, flanken or other
    soup beef, trimmed and
    cut up
1 medium-sized yam,
    peeled and sliced thin
4 small red or white boiling
    potatoes, unpeeled and
    sliced thin
2 medium-sized beets,
    peeled and coarsely
    grated
1 onion, sliced thin
2 carrots, sliced thin
1 leek or 3 scallions, tender
    greens included, sliced
    thin
1 medium-sized turnip,

    peeled and diced
½ head small cabbage, in
    1-inch chunks
½ cup chopped parsley
1 10½-ounce can condensed
    beef bouillon
1 8-ounce can tomato sauce
¼ cup light brown sugar
3 tablespoons cider vinegar
2 teaspoons salt
Freshly ground pepper to
    taste
¾ teaspoon dill
5½ cups broth made from
    beef bouillon powder or
    cubes
Sour cream or plain yogurt

Combine all ingredients except sour cream in crock, using only enough broth to come to 1 inch of top. Stir gently to mix well. Cover and cook 10 hours on Low. Turn into warmed soup tureen and thin with heated remaining broth. Adjust seasonings. Pass sour cream to stir into each serving. Borshch keeps in the refrigerator up to 4 or 5 days and is excellent cold. *Makes 12 servings.*

❦

ONION SOUP

Serve the broth plain one day and add onions the next. Both soups are delicious.

2 pounds meaty beef shank, shin, neck, or other soup beef, trimmed
1 stalk celery, including leaves, coarsely chopped
1 carrot, coarsely chopped
½ bay leaf
2 whole cloves
8 peppercorns
1 teaspoon salt

4 cups water
3 large onions, thinly sliced
1 small clove garlic, minced
3 tablespoons butter or margarine
2 teaspoons Worcestershire sauce
6 thick slices toasted and buttered French bread
Grated Parmesan cheese

Add beef to crock with celery, carrot, bay leaf, cloves, peppercorns, salt and water. Cover and cook 10 hours on Low. Refrigerate up to 2 days.* Pour soup through sieve into crock, set on Low. (Use beef for another meal.) Sauté onions and garlic in butter without browning until limp. Stir into beef broth and add Worcestershire sauce. Cover and cook 4 hours. Adjust seasonings. Ladle from crock over a slice of toasted French bread in each soup bowl. Sprinkle with Parmesan cheese and serve. *Makes 6 servings.*

— ❦ —

TURKEY SOUP CREOLE

2 pounds turkey wings
4 whole scallions, coarsely
   chopped
1 large carrot, finely
   chopped
1 large stalk celery, leaves
   included, finely chopped
½ cup chopped parsley
½ cup uncooked long grain
   rice
2 cups beef broth

2 cups chicken broth
1 bay leaf, crumbled
¼ teaspoon thyme
1 teaspoon salt
¼ teaspoon freshly ground
   pepper
1 tablespoon each softened
   margarine and flour
¾ cup half-and-half or
   cream
Croutons

Disjoint wings and remove and discard tips. Combine scallions, carrot, celery, parsley and rice. In crock, layer vegetables and turkey wings, beginning and ending with vegetables. Mix broths, bay leaf, thyme, salt and pepper. Pour into crock. Liquid should cover by about 1 inch. Cover and cook 8 hours on Low. Remove soup to bowl and let cool. Lift out meat, discard skin and bones and chop meat in fairly small dice. Purée remaining soup. Rub margarine and flour together, blend into soup. Add half-and-half. Taste for seasoning. Stir in diced turkey. Reheat in crock without simmering or refrigerate up to 2 days and then reheat and serve. Serve with croutons. *Makes 8–10 servings.*

❧

MEXICAN MEATBALLS IN BROTH

Special here is the zucchini, which makes the meat moist and gives it flavor.

1 pound lean ground beef
½ pound lean ground pork
1 medium-large zucchini, finely chopped
1 large onion, finely chopped
2 eggs
2 tablespoons uncooked rice
1 teaspoon chili powder
½ teaspoon oregano
½ teaspoon ground cumin seed
¾ teaspoon salt
¼ teaspoon freshly ground pepper

1 clove garlic, minced
2 tablespoons oil
2 large tomatoes (fresh or canned), drained and chopped
¼ cup chopped parsley
1½ cups condensed beef consommé
2 tablespoons lemon juice
2½ cups water
Chopped cilantro or parsley
Sour cream
1 cup cooked rice (optional)

Blend meats together in bowl. Mix zucchini, ⅓ of the onion, eggs, rice, ½ teaspoon of the chili powder, oregano, cumin, salt and pepper into meat, shape in walnut-sized balls and refrigerate. Lightly brown remaining onion with garlic in oil. Add tomatoes and sauté 2 or 3 minutes. Mix in remaining ½ teaspoon chili powder and the parsley, consommé, lemon juice and 2½ cups water. Turn into crock. Drop meatballs into broth, cover and cook about 3 hours on Low or until cooked. Adjust seasoning. Serve sprinkled with chopped cilantro and dolloped with sour cream.

To make this soup even more filling, stir in about 1 cup cooked rice before serving, if you wish. Or serve the broth and rice as a first course and save the meatballs for a main course. *Makes 5 dozen meatballs. Allow 6–8 per serving.*

SILKY BEEF SOUP

1 onion, finely chopped
1 large carrot, finely chopped
1 large stalk celery, including leaves, finely chopped
1 parsnip, peeled and finely chopped
1 clove garlic, minced
½ cup chopped parsley
½ bay leaf
3 pounds meaty cross-cut

beef shank, neck, flanken or other soup beef, trimmed
1 teaspoon salt
¼ teaspoon freshly ground pepper or to taste
1 46-ounce can tomato juice or vegetable cocktail
Plain yogurt, sour cream, or grated Parmesan cheese (optional)

Mix onion, carrot, celery, parsnip, garlic, parsley and bay leaf. Make layers of vegetables and beef in crock, lightly sprinkling with salt and pepper. Pour juice over layers and shake crock to distribute. Cover and cook 14 hours on Low. Turn soup into warmed tureen. Remove meat and pull out bones. Coarsely chop meat and return to soup. Adjust seasoning. A little yogurt, sour cream or grated Parmesan cheese makes it heartier. *Makes 6–8 servings.*

❦

GUMBO

1 large onion, chopped
1 clove garlic, minced
2 tablespoons oil
½ green pepper, chopped
   fine
1 28-ounce can Italian-
   style tomatoes, broken up
12 ounces lean ham, in
   ½-inch pieces
½ cup chopped parsley
2 pounds chicken pieces
1 teaspoon salt
Freshly ground pepper
1 13¾-ounce can chicken

broth or equivalent from
   powder
1 10-ounce package frozen
   okra, cut or whole
8 ounces small cleaned
   shrimp (fresh, frozen,
   canned, raw or cooked)
1 8-ounce can whole oysters
1½ teaspoons filé powder,
   or substitute ½ teaspoon
   ground thyme and 1
   crumbled bay leaf
Hot cooked rice

Sauté onion and garlic in oil until golden. Add green pepper, tomatoes, ham and parsley and mix well. Remove skin and fat from chicken. In crock, layer skillet ingredients with chicken, beginning and ending with vegetables. Lightly season with salt and pepper as you go. Add broth. Cover, cook 4 hours on Low. Thaw okra, add with shrimp and oysters, including oyster broth. Cover and cook 3 hours more. Turn into warmed tureen. Remove bones from chicken, stir in filé powder. Taste for seasoning. Serve at once over rice. Do not reheat after filé powder has been added or soup will get stringy. *Makes 6–8 servings.*

NOTE: Fresh crab, jumbo prawns, minced clams, and smoked sausage links may be substituted for any or several of the gumbo ingredients.

MENUDO
(MEXICAN TRIPE SOUP)

If tripe has not been steamed before purchase, dice, cover with water in crock and cook on Low about 12 hours. Drain and continue with recipe.

2 pounds tripe, in ½-inch
  dice, no fat
1 16-ounce can hominy,
  drained
1 large onion, finely
  chopped
2 large cloves garlic,
  minced
1 pound veal shank,
  knuckle or neck, cut in
  1-inch slices by butcher
⅓ cup (2 ounces) finely
  chopped mild green chilies
6 tablespoons tomato purée
  or sauce
½ teaspoon oregano
1 teaspoon salt
¼ teaspoon freshly ground
  pepper or to taste
Chopped cilantro, parsley,
  or mint leaves
Chopped scallions

Put in the crock the tripe, hominy, onion, garlic, veal, chilies, tomato purée, oregano, salt and pepper. Add 6 cups water and mix well. Cover and cook on Low about 14 hours, or until tripe is tender. Taste for seasoning. Remove bones. Remove fat from top, chilling soup first if you have time. Sprinkle with cilantro and scallions. Serve with warm tortillas and taco sauce, if you wish. *Makes 6 servings.*

❦

BARBADOS PEPPER POT

This is as much stew as soup. Serve it as a one-pot dinner, or serve the broth first and the meats after.

2 pounds oxtails, trimmed and cut in sections
2 pounds boneless pork shoulder, trimmed and cut in 1¼-inch chunks
8 ounces salt pork, cut in slivers
2 pounds chicken pieces
Oil
1 large carrot, cut in thin ½-inch sticks
1 large onion, thinly sliced

1 clove garlic, minced
1 teaspoon salt
⅛ teaspoon freshly ground pepper
⅛ teaspoon curry powder (optional)
1½ teaspoons bottled gravy coloring
3 cups chicken broth
2 whole dried small red chili peppers

Using the same large, heavy skillet and leaving the drippings in the pan, brown each meat and the chicken separately. Sauté carrot, onion and garlic in skillet until golden. Sprinkle with salt, pepper and curry and stir. Layer meats and chicken in crock, sprinkling with vegetables as you go. Combine gravy coloring with broth in skillet and pour over crock, scraping skillet well. Bury unbroken chili pods (seeds must stay inside) in meat. Cover and cook 8 hours on Low until tender. Adjust seasonings, remove chili peppers, skim off fat, and serve. *Makes 6–8 servings.*

❦

TRIPLE-STRENGTH CHICKEN STOCK

Collect chicken trimmings and the giblet packages that come with whole chickens and keep them in the freezer until you have a crockful. Then simply layer them in the crock and wait for it to work its magic. The stock is so concentrated that it may be diluted with water to three times its volume.

> 5 pounds fat-free chicken
> trimmings—giblets, necks,
> backs, wing tips, skin and
> bones
> 1 or 2 carrots, thinly sliced
> 1 or 2 stalks celery, leaves
> included, thinly sliced
> 1 onion, thinly sliced
> 2 or 3 cloves garlic, thinly
> sliced
>
> 1 parsnip (optional), thinly
> sliced
> 1 small turnip (optional),
> thinly sliced
> ½ cup chopped parsley
> Freshly ground pepper to
> taste
> Salt
> ½ bay leaf
> ½ teaspoon thyme

Mix carrots, celery, onion, garlic, parsnip, turnip and parsley. Layer chicken trimmings in crock alternately with layers of vegetables, lightly seasoning with salt and pepper as you go. Add bay and thyme on top. Cover and cook 24 hours on Low, or until crock is filled with stock. Wring out a clean cloth, spread in a large sieve or colander over a bowl. Ladle contents of crock into it. When cool, wring every drop of stock from bundle into the bowl. Chill and lift off fat. Refrigerate or freeze. *Makes 1 generous quart*. Dilute with 2 parts water to 1 part stock to make broth.

❦

BROTH FROM BONES

Use this basic recipe for the leftover bones of any meat or poultry.

> Carcass from 1 10-pound
> turkey
> 1 onion, sliced
> 1 carrot, sliced
> 1 stalk celery with leaves,
> sliced
>
> Few sprigs parsley
> Salt
> Freshly ground pepper
> Cooked rice or noodles
> Chopped parsley

Using a meat cleaver, break up the bones of the turkey carcass to fit the crock. Add the onion, carrot, celery, parsley, salt and pepper. Cover with cold water to 1 inch of the top of the crock. Cover and cook on High until it simmers, then turn to Low and cook overnight, or until the flavor is good. Strain and adjust seasonings. Serve with rice or noodles and chopped parsley.

Seven

❦

GROUND MEATS

❧

COOKING GROUND MEATS IN THE CROCK

Shape	*Setting/Hours*

CASSEROLES

with blanched pasta and basically cooked ingredients, ⅔ full	· HIGH: 1½ or Low: 3
in custard	· HIGH: 1¾
with unthawed frozen or blanched fresh vegetables	· HIGH: 2 or Low: 4
basically cooked ingredients but densely layered or ¾ full	· HIGH: 2 or Low: 4
mixed with uncooked rice, ⅔ full	· HIGH: 2 or Low: 4
mixed with uncooked rice, ¾ full	· HIGH: 2¼ or Low: 4½
basically cooked ingredients blending flavors, ¾ full	· Low: 4½
with uncooked fresh vegetables, not sautéed, finely chopped	· HIGH: 2½ or Low: 5
with dried vegetables reconstituted in crock	· HIGH: 2½ or Low: 5

MEAT LOAVES

with or without blanched or finely cut vegetables	· HIGH: 2¼ or Low: 4½

MEATBALLS

baked in sauce	· Low: 4

Shape	Setting/Hours
STUFFED LEAVES	
grape leaves ·	Low: 10
cabbage leaves ·	High: 8 then Low: 5

MEAT AND VEGETABLES MACEDONIA

1 clove garlic, minced
1 onion, finely chopped
1 15-ounce can tomato
  sauce
¼ cup dry white wine
1½ teaspoons basil
16 ounces (4 cups) frozen
  potato nuggets
1 pound lean ground beef
  or lamb (or 2 cups
  chopped, cooked meats)

1 16-ounce can white beans,
  drained
¼ small head green
  cabbage, finely chopped
½ large green pepper,
  finely chopped
1 tablespoon salt
Freshly ground pepper
Grated Parmesan cheese

Mix garlic with onion. Blend tomato sauce, wine and basil. In oiled crock, layer potatoes, meat, onion, beans, meat, cabbage, green pepper, potatoes. Lightly season each layer with salt and pepper and moisten with sauce as you go. Cover.* Cook 5 hours on Low or about 2½ hours on High. Turn into serving dish, gently stirring to blend. Top each serving with Parmesan cheese. *Makes 8 servings.*

CASSEROLE WITH ARTICHOKE HEARTS

Frozen potato nuggets are the rare frozen potato processed without preservatives. They can be counted upon to bake quickly in the crock whereas even the finest shred of raw potato will take ages.

1 pound ground beef, lamb, veal, turkey, lean sausage (or 2 cups chopped, cooked meats, ham or chicken)
Oil
2 tablespoons dried onion flakes
¾ teaspoon salt or to taste
Dash of cinnamon
2 6-ounce cans white sauce
6 tablespoons grated Parmesan cheese
¼ teaspoon nutmeg
Dash of white pepper
1 9-ounce package frozen artichoke hearts
16 ounces (generous 4 cups) frozen potato nuggets
¼ cup (3 ounces) chopped pimientos
Paprika
Grated Parmesan cheese

Brown ground meat lightly in skillet, using oil only if necessary. Drain off fat. Mix in onion flakes, salt and cinnamon. (Or simply add these to cooked meat.) Blend white sauce, Parmesan, nutmeg and white pepper. Separate unthawed artichoke hearts. Fold ⅓ sauce into them. In oiled crock make a layer each of unthawed potato nuggets, meat, pimientos and artichoke hearts, repeating once. Smooth remaining sauce over top. Dust with paprika and Parmesan cheese. Cover and cook about 2 hours on High or about 4 hours on Low, or until bubbling hot. Serve from crock. *Makes 6 servings.*

🌷

CROSS CREEK CASSEROLE

Generous 4 cups (8 ounces) noodles (not fine)
1 tablespoon oil
1½ pounds ground beef, veal, turkey, lean sausage (or 2–3 cups chopped, cooked meats, ham or chicken)
Oil
½ teaspoon salt or to taste
1 8-ounce can tomato sauce
1 cup cottage cheese
1 cup condensed cream of mushroom or cream of onion soup
6 whole scallions, chopped fine
1 clove garlic, minced
Chopped parsley

Boil noodles in water for about 3 minutes, or only until they lose their raw look. Drain and toss with oil. Brown ground meat lightly in skillet, using oil only if necessary; drain off fat. Mix in salt and tomato sauce. (Or simply add to cooked meat.) In blender or food processor blend cottage cheese and soup. In oiled crock make a layer each of noodles, scallions and garlic, cottage cheese mixture and meat, repeating once. Layer remaining noodles, scallions and sauce. Cover.* Cook about 1½ hours on High or about 3 hours on Low, or until bubbling hot. Serve from crock, dusted with parsley. *Makes 6–8 servings.*

❦

CREAMY MEAT AND MACARONI CASSEROLE

1 cup elbow macaroni
1 10½-ounce can cheese
  sauce
2 onions, chopped
1 green pepper, chopped
2 cloves garlic, minced
3 tablespoons oil
1 pound ground beef, lean
  sausage, turkey (or 2 cups
  chopped, cooked meats,
  ham or chicken)

1 8-ounce can tomato sauce
½ cup thick plain yogurt
  or sour cream
2 teaspoons lemon juice
1 teaspoon chili powder
1 teaspoon oregano
½ teaspoon salt
Freshly ground pepper
Grated Parmesan cheese

Cook marcaroni in boiling water 4 minutes. Drain. Mix with cheese sauce. Lightly brown onions, green pepper and garlic in oil. Add ground meat and brown lightly; drain off fat. (Or simply add cooked meat to skillet.) Blend in tomato sauce, yogurt, lemon juice, chili powder, oregano, salt and pepper. In oiled crock layer meat and macaroni, beginning and ending with meat. Dust top with Parmesan cheese and cover.* Cook about 1½ hours on High, or about 3 hours on Low, or until bubbling hot. Serve from crock. *Makes 6–8 servings.*

❦

LAYERED ENCHILADAS

2 small green peppers,
  finely chopped
2 onions, finely chopped
3 cloves garlic, minced
3 to 4 tablespoons oil
2 pounds ground beef or
  poultry (or 4 cups
  chopped, cooked meats)
1 tablespoon chili powder
  or to taste

1¼ teaspoons salt
8 ounces cream cheese
1 10¾-ounce can condensed
  cream of onion soup
1 tablespoon lemon juice
5 7-inch corn tortillas
3 cups shredded mild
  cheese

Lightly brown green peppers, onions and garlic in oil. Add ground meat and brown lightly; drain off fat. (Or simply add cooked meat to skillet.) Mix in chili powder and salt. In blender or food processor blend cream cheese, soup and lemon juice. In oiled crock make a layer each of tortilla, meat, shredded cheese and cream cheese mixture, repeating 4 times. Cover.* Cook about 2 hours on High or about 4 hours on Low. Serve from crock. *Makes 8–10 servings.*

❦

RICE AND MEAT

Be careful not to overcook.

1 large onion, chopped
½ green pepper, chopped
2 cloves garlic, minced
3 tablespoons oil
1¼ cups uncooked rice
1½ teaspoons oregano
2 teaspoons salt
1 teaspoon chili powder or
*   to taste*
1¼ pounds ground beef,
*   turkey, or lean sausage*
Oil

1 12-ounce can corn,
*   drained*
1 4¼-ounce can chopped
*   or sliced black olives,*
*   drained*
½ cup raisins
1 16-ounce jar Italian
*   cooking sauce or thick-*
*   quality tomato sauce*
5 ounces canned beef gravy
Sour cream
Cilantro or parsley, freshly
*   chopped*

Sauté onion, green pepper and garlic in 2 tablespoons oil until softened. Add 1 tablespoon oil and rice. Sauté until rice is clear. Remove from heat. Add oregano, 1 teaspoon salt and chili powder. Turn into crock. Lightly brown ground meat in skillet, using oil only if necessary; drain off fat. Add corn, olives, raisins, tomato sauce, 1 teaspoon salt and gravy. Blend with rice in crock. Do not overmix or pack down. Cover.° Cook 2¼ hours on High or 4½ hours on Low. Stir gently, then serve garnished with sour cream and fresh cilantro or parsley. *Makes 10 servings.*

❧

SFOGATO
(GREEK MEAT AND VEGETABLE CUSTARD)

2 onions, chopped
2 tablespoons oil
1 tablespoon margarine
3 zucchini, finely chopped
1 pound ground beef, veal,
  lamb, lean sausage, turkey
  (or 2 cups chopped
  cooked meats, ham or
  chicken)
2 fresh tomatoes, peeled
  and chopped

Small bunch parsley,
  chopped
Pinch of mint
Pinch of cinnamon
1 teaspoon salt
4 eggs
½ cup beef broth
¼ cup grated Parmesan
  cheese
Freshly ground pepper

Sauté onions in oil and margarine in large skillet until soft. Add zucchini and sauté 2 to 3 minutes more. Add ground meat, brown until still slightly pink; drain off fat. (Or simply add cooked meat to skillet.) Add tomatoes, parsley, mint, cinnamon and salt. Remove from heat. Beat eggs and broth until blended. Gently stir into skillet. Turn into crock and stir to blend. Dust with Parmesan cheese and pepper. Cover and cook 1¾ hours on High. Serve from crock. *Makes 6 servings.*

— ❦ —

SHEPHERD'S PIE

6 medium potatoes, peeled
and cooked
6 tablespoons butter or
margarine
6 tablespoons milk
½ teaspoon salt or to taste
Freshly ground white
pepper to taste
1 pound ground lamb, beef
or turkey (or 2 cups
chopped cooked meats)
Oil
2 tomatoes, peeled and
chopped
1 whole scallion, finely
chopped

Small bunch parsley, finely
chopped
1 cup thinly sliced carrots,
cooked
1 cup frozen small
peas
1 cup canned mushroom or
thick homemade beef
gravy
1 teaspoon Worcestershire
sauce
Pinch of garlic powder
Butter or margarine

Purée potatoes and whip with margarine, milk, salt and pepper. Brown ground meat lightly in skillet, adding oil only if necessary; drain off fat. Add tomatoes, scallion, parsley, carrots, unthawed peas, gravy, Worcestershire sauce and garlic powder and mix together gently. Turn into crock. Spoon potatoes over top, swirling to cover. Dot with margarine and cover.* Bake 2 hours on High or 4 hours on Low. Serve from crock. *Makes 6–8 servings.*

❧

CHILI CON CARNE

2 large onions, chopped
4 cloves garlic, minced
3–4 tablespoons oil
½ cup chili powder or to
  taste
2¼ pounds coarsely ground
  beef or half beef and pork
Scant 2 teaspoons salt
2 tablespoons beef boullion
  powder
½ teaspoon ground cumin
  seed

1 15-ounce can tomato
  sauce
2 15-ounce cans or 3 cups
  cooked pink or small red
  beans, drained
1 16-ounce can tomato
  wedges, coarsely
  chopped with juice
Chopped raw onions
  (optional)

Brown onions and garlic in oil. Stir in chili powder and sauté until blended. Remove from pan. Add meat and brown lightly; drain off fat. Mix in salt, bouillon powder, cumin, tomato sauce, beans and tomatoes. Add browned onions last. Do not overmix. Cover.* Cook 4½ hours on Low. Remove fat. Adjust seasoning. Serve from crock, garnishing each portion with chopped raw onion, if desired. *Makes 8–10 servings.*

NOTE: The meat will make or break this chili. Don't buy regular ground beef or let the butcher urge a "chili-grind" of round on you. Choose about a 3½-pound blade or 7-bone chuck roast with some fat on it and ask the butcher to grind it once. A little pork adds flavor but it might be too rich for some tastes.

❧

RED FLANNEL HASH

Layered in the crock and simply stirred before serving, hash bakes to a perfect texture. For crisp edges, brown briefly.

1 large onion, chopped
1 tablespoon oil
4 potatoes (4 cups), peeled,
    cooked and diced
2 cups chopped roast or
    boiled beef, cooked corned
    beef or pastrami

1 cup finely chopped
    pickled beets
1¼ teaspoons salt or to taste
Freshly ground pepper
Margarine
Chopped parsley or dill
Horseradish (optional)

Lightly brown onions in oil. In oiled crock layer potatoes, onions, meat, potatoes, beets, meat, potatoes. Lightly season layers with salt and pepper as you go. Dot top with margarine and cover.* Cook 2 hours on High or 4 hours on Low. Stir gently. Serve from crock garnished with parsley and accompanied with horseradish, if you wish. *Makes 6 servings.*

QUICK HASH AND CABBAGE

1 firm medium-sized
    green cabbage, finely
    shredded
3 tablespoons butter or
    margarine
2 onions, chopped
3 tablespoons oil

2 tablespoons dill or
    caraway seeds
½ teaspoon paprika
2 16-ounce cans or 4 cups
    homemade hash
About ½ cup chili sauce
Sour cream or plain yogurt

Cover cabbage with boiling water for 5 minutes; drain. Mix in margarine. Brown onions lightly in oil in large skillet. Add cabbage and sauté 2 or 3 minutes more. Mix in seeds and paprika. In oiled crock layer cabbage and hash, beginning and ending with cabbage. Top with chili sauce and cover.* Cook 1½ hours on High or 3 hours on Low. Serve from crock, dolloped with sour cream. *Makes 8 servings.*

—————— ❧ ——————

KITCHEN GARDEN MEAT LOAF

Add other vegetables—zucchini, green peppers, okra, shredded cabbage—if you have them, but keep them 2 inches below the top of the crock.

1 onion, grated
Small bunch parsley,
chopped
2 pounds lean ground beef
or other meat
4 eggs
2 cups soft bread crumbs,
cooked oatmeal or cooked
rice
1⅔ cups buttermilk or milk
2 teaspoons lemon juice
1–2 teaspoons salt
¼ teaspoon freshly ground
pepper
1 teaspoon bottled gravy
coloring

1–2 small turnips or other
vegetable, cut in match-
stick-sized strips
4–8 carrots, cut in match-
stick-sized strips
2 to 4 stalks celery, cut in
matchstick-sized strips
2 tablespoons oil
1 16-ounce can stewed or
plain tomatoes, drained
and broken up
1 cup sour cream or plain
yogurt to taste

Blend onion, parsley, eggs, bread crumbs, buttermilk, lemon juice, 1 teaspoon salt and pepper lightly but thoroughly into meat. Mixture will be soft. Cook a bit in dry skillet and taste for seasoning. Pack in crock. Brush with coloring. Cover, start cooking on High. Sauté turnips, carrots and celery in oil until softened and lightly browned. Stir in tomatoes and a little salt. Pour over meat in crock and cover.* Cook 2¼ hours on High, counting from when you began. Remove meat and vegetables to warmed serving platter. Blend sour cream into crock juices. Adjust seasonings. Turn into bowl and pass separately. *Makes 8 servings.*

❧

TURKEY LOAF WITH ZUCCHINI

1 16-ounce can stewed
  tomatoes
4 slices home-style
  bread
1 pound ground turkey
1 pound lean ground beef
1 egg
About 2 teaspoons salt
¼ teaspoon freshly ground
  pepper

1 or 2 scallions, chopped
1 clove garlic, minced
6 good-sized (1½ pounds)
  zucchini, in ¼-inch
  slices
Olive oil
¼ cup grated Parmesan
  cheese

Drain juice from tomatoes into mixing bowl. Crumble in bread, break up lightly with fork. Lightly but thoroughly blend in meats, egg, 1½ teaspoon salt and ⅛ teaspoon pepper. Lightly pack in crock. Mix scallions, garlic and tomotoes. Layer tomatoes and zucchini over meat, sprinkling with a little oil, salt and pepper. Sprinkle top with Parmesan and cover.* Cook 4½ hours on Low or 2¼ hours on High. Remove meat and vegetables to warmed serving platter. *Makes 8 servings.*

❦

UN-STUFFED CABBAGE

Make this a day ahead, if you wish. It is excellent reheated the next day.

2 pounds green cabbage
1 pound sauerkraut
(preferably not canned)
2 onions, 1 coarsely
chopped, 1 finely
chopped
1 clove garlic, minced
Generous ½ teaspoon
paprika
1 tablespoon salt
1½ pounds lean ground
beef

Generous ½ cup uncooked
rice
1 egg
2 tablespoons chopped
parsley
¾ teaspoon dill
⅛ teaspoon freshly
ground pepper
About ⅓ cup hot water
1 15-ounce can tomato
sauce
3 cups sour cream
Paprika

Cut core out of cabbage, set in deep bowl and cover with boiling water. When cool, drain and chop. Drain sauerkraut, rinse under cold water and squeeze out excess moisture. Toss cabbage, coarsely chopped onion, garlic, sauerkraut, paprika and 2 teaspoons salt together. Mix meat with finely chopped onion, rice, egg, parsley, dill, pepper and scant 1 teaspoon salt. Add enough of the hot water to make mixture light. Arrange a quarter of the cabbage on bottom of crock. Shape meat into a round 2 inches smaller than crock. Set it in. Fill around and over meat with remaining cabbage. Pour tomato sauce over and cover.° Cook 10 to 11 hours on Low or 2½ hours on High, and then 5 to 6 hours on Low. Remove meat to warmed deep platter. Use slotted spoon to arrange cabbage around it. Slice meat in 8 or 10 wedges, overlap in circle. Whisk generous ½ cup sour cream into crock juices. Adjust seasoning. Pour over platter. Dust with paprika. Pass remaining sour cream. *Makes 8–10 servings.*

LAMB LOAF

1½ pounds lean ground
  lamb
2 cloves garlic, minced
½ cup very finely
  chopped onions
½ cup very finely
  chopped celery
½ cup very finely
  chopped carrots
6 tablespoons hamburger
  relish

2 tablespoons prepared
  mustard
1 cup seasoned bread
  crumbs
1½ teaspoons salt
¼ teaspoon freshly ground
  pepper
1 egg
¾ cup plain yogurt
1 teaspoon gravy coloring
¼ cup catsup

Lightly but thoroughly combine lamb, garlic, onions, celery, carrots, relish, mustard, crumbs, salt, pepper, egg and yogurt. Pack in crock. Brush with gravy coloring. Spread top with catsup and cover.* Cook 4½ hours on Low or 2¼ hours on High. Serve from crock or remove to warmed serving platter. Adjust seasoning and spoon crock juices over loaf. *Makes 6 servings.*

ITALIAN MEATBALLS

1 clove garlic, minced
1½ pounds lean ground
  beef
½ cup minced fresh
  spinach, chard or beet
  leaves
⅓ cup grated Romano or
  Parmesan cheese
¼ cup dry bread crumbs
¼ cup minced parsley
1 teaspoon basil

1 teaspoon freshly ground
  pepper
¼ teaspoon salt
Pinch of nutmeg
3 eggs
6–8 tablespoons ice water
2 quarts Italian-style
  tomato sauce
Splash dry red wine
  (optional)
Cooked pasta or rice

Lightly but thoroughly combine garlic, beef, spinach, cheese, crumbs, parsley, basil, pepper, salt, nutmeg and eggs. Add just enough of the ice water to make mixture fluffy. Blend sauce with wine, if used. Turn into crock. Shape meat into walnut-sized balls. Drop into crock as you go, pushing beneath sauce. Cover.* Cook 4 hours on Low. They will hold on Low for a few hours if necessary. Skim off fat. Adjust seasoning. Serve over pasta or rice. *Makes about 42 meatballs; allow 6–8 per serving.*

———————— 🌷 ————————

SWEET AND SOUR MEATBALLS

1 small onion, finely
   chopped
1½ pounds lean ground
   beef
½ cup bread crumbs
1½ teaspoons salt
¼ teaspoon ground
   ginger
2½ tablespoons lemon
   juice
About 1 cup ice water
8 gingersnap cookies,
   crushed

1 10½-ounce can con-
   densed onion soup
¼ cup beef broth
3 tablespoons catsup
1 tablespoon cider vinegar
1 tablespoon brown sugar
½ cup raisins
Freshly ground pepper
Buttered noodles

Lightly mix the onion, beef, bread crumbs, salt, ginger, 2 tablespoons lemon juice, and just enough ice water to make the mixture fluffy. Shape into walnut-sized meatballs. Brown them in an ungreased skillet. Blend gingersnaps with ½ tablespoon lemon juice, onion soup, beef broth, catsup, vinegar, sugar, raisins and pepper. Layer meatballs in crock, moistening thoroughly with sauce. Cover.* Cook 4 hours on Low. Skim off fat. Adjust seasoning. Serve over buttered egg noodles. *Makes about 54 meatballs; allow 6–8 per serving.*

If necessary, you can hold these on Low for a few hours.

❦

NIPPY MEATBALLS IN MUSHROOM SAUCE

Makes a large batch for a party or to freeze for several meals.

1 onion, finely chopped
2 tablespoons oil
2 pounds lean ground beef
1 pound lean ground pork
4 eggs
1 cup seasoned bread crumbs
1 12-ounce bottle beer
1 tablespoon dill
1 teaspoon salt

1 teaspoon freshly ground pepper
1 4-ounce can mushrooms pieces and stems, drained
1 10½-ounce can condensed cream of mushroom soup
2 tablespoons lemon juice
Chopped parsley

Lightly brown onion in oil. Mix meats with onion, eggs, bread crumbs, beer, dill, salt and pepper. Shape into walnut-sized meatballs. Brown in ungreased skillet. Blend mushrooms with undiluted soup and lemon juice. Layer meatballs in crock, moistening thoroughly with sauce, and cover.* Cook 4 hours on Low. Skim off fat. Adjust seasoning. Remove to warmed serving bowl and sprinkle with parsley. *Makes 9½ dozen meatballs; allow 6–8 per serving.*

MEATBALLS JAVA
WITH JAPANESE-STYLE RICE

*1 large red onion, finely
  chopped*
2 tablespoons oil
*1 large whole scallion,
  chopped*
1 pound lean ground beef
1 teaspoon curry powder
1 teaspoon ground cumin
*½ teaspoon ground
  coriander*
⅛ teaspoon chili powder
⅛ teaspoon cayenne
1 teaspoon salt

*1 20-ounce can pineapple
  chunks, drained (save
  juice)*
*1 large tomato, peeled and
  chopped*
1 tablespoon cornstarch
*1 teaspoon bottled gravy
  coloring*
1 teaspoon sugar
*Chopped peanuts or
  macadamia nuts*
Coconut
*Japanese-style Rice (see
  below)*

Sauté onion in oil until softened. Mix onion, scallion, beef, spices and salt. Shape into walnut-sized meatballs. Mix pineapple with tomato. Gently mix meatballs and pineapple in crock. Pour juice over and cover.* Cook 4 hours on Low. Lift meatballs and pineapple into warmed serving dish. Turn juices into skillet and skim off fat. Blend a little cooled broth with cornstarch and whisk into sauce over medium heat until thickened. Add gravy coloring and sugar and adjust seasoning. Stir into meatballs. Garnish with chopped nuts and coconut, toasted if you like. *Makes 5 servings.* Serve with Japanese-style Rice.

JAPANESE-STYLE RICE

1 cup short- or medium-grain rice

ning water until water in bowl is clear. Place rice in deep pot Turn rice into sieve, set over bowl and shake under cold run-

and cover with cold water by 1 inch. Do not add salt. Soak 1 to 2 hours. Set over highest heat, tightly covered, and listen for full boil. Reduce heat at once to very low and simmer exactly 12 minutes. Turn off heat, let stand 5 minutes or longer before serving. *Makes 5 servings.*

NOTE: If cooking more than 3 cups rice, simmer 15 minutes.

❦

SWEET AND SOUR CABBAGE ROLLS

Blanch the cabbage well, or the rolls will take forever to cook.

2 *small firm heads cabbage*	¼ *cup lemon juice*
2 *onions, finely chopped*	2 *tablespoons brown sugar*
2 *teaspoons salt*	1 *teaspoon cider vinegar*
Freshly ground pepper	1 *pound lean ground beef*
1 *28-ounce can tomatoes,*	¼ *cup uncooked rice*
broken up	1 *egg*
⅔ *cup apricot preserves*	3 *cups sour cream*
1 *cup currants (optional)*	

Cut cores from cabbages. Set in deep bowl and cover with boiling water. When cool, drain, saving ½ cup water. Set aside 15 largest leaves. Pare down thick spines. Finely chop remaining cabbage. Mix half the onions with cabbage, 1 teaspoon salt and a little pepper and set aside. Make sauce by mixing tomatoes and their juice with preserves, currants, lemon juice, brown sugar, vinegar, ½ teaspoon salt and a little pepper. Mix remaining onions with ½ teaspoon salt, a little pepper and the beef, rice, egg and cabbage water. Arrange 1-inch-thick rolls of meat along the base of each cabbage leaf, leaving 1-inch margins on both sides. Fold 1 margin over, roll up loosely, and tuck other margin into itself. In crock, make a layer each of chopped cabbage, sauce and cabbage rolls, repeating 3 times. Cover.* Set crock in large pan to catch overflow. Cook 8 hours on High, then about 5 hours on Low or until cabbage is cooked. Remove rolls and cabbage to baking dish. Whisk 1 cup sour cream into crock juices. Pour over rolls. Cover with waxed paper and refrigerate up to 5 days; they will improve each day. Reheat covered with foil at 350° about 1½ hours. Adjust seasoning. Serve with lots of sour cream. *Makes 15 rolls; allow 2–3 per serving.*

❧

STUFFED GRAPE LEAVES

1 pound ground beef
⅔ cup uncooked rice
3½ cups simmering beef
  broth
1 teaspoon salt
¼ cup currants or raisins
⅛ teaspoon mint
⅛ teaspoon freshly ground
  pepper

1 jar (approximately 60)
  grape leaves in brine
3 tablespoons tomato purée
1 tablespoon lemon juice
Olive oil
Thin lemon slices

Brown ground beef in ungreased skillet until slightly pink. Drain off fat. Add rice and sauté 2 or 3 minutes more. Stir in 1½ cups beef broth, cover and simmer gently 15 minutes or until rice is tender but not fully cooked. Stir in salt, currants, mint and pepper. Cool. Drain leaves. Dip each in hot water and clip off stems. Lay leaves shiny side down, base toward you. Arrange about 1 tablespoon meat in thin roll along base, leaving margins on both sides. Fold 1 margin over, roll leaf up loosely, tuck other margin into itself, sealing roll. Each roll should be 1 by 2 inches. Layer rolls in crock, using about 12 each layer. Use torn leaves between each layer and to cover top. Blend tomato purée, lemon juice and 2 cups broth. Pour over crock. Drizzle top with olive oil. Lay a plate on top to keep rolls in place and cover.* Cook 10 hours on Low. Remove rolls with tongs to serving platter. Adjust seasoning, then pour crock juices over the rolls. Garnish with lemon slices. Serve hot, cool or cold. *Makes 50 rolls; allow 4–6 per serving.*

Stuffed grape leaves will keep in the refrigerator up to 6 days.

Eight

❦

BEEF

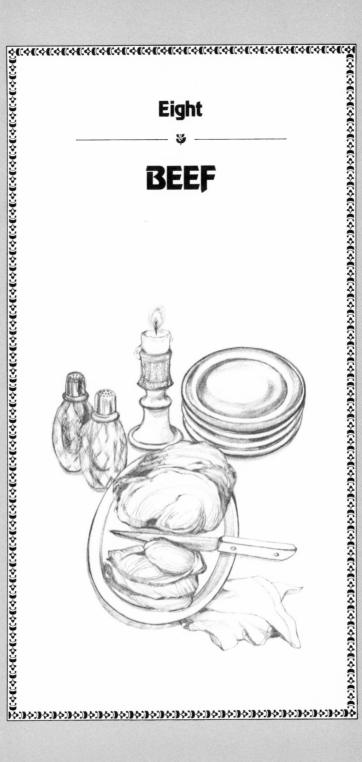

COOKING BEEF IN THE CROCK

Shape	Setting/Hours
BRAISED	
inch-thick strips ·	HIGH: 2½ or LOW: 5
½-inch by 3-inch strips ·	LOW: 5–5½
3-pound corned beef round or brisket ·	HIGH: 5½
stuffed tenderized round steak ·	HIGH: ¼ then LOW: 5¾–6
1-inch chunks with basically cooked vegetables ·	LOW: 7
1½-inch chunks marinated with vegetables ·	LOW: 8–9
stuffed flank steak ·	LOW: 8½
1½-inch chunks with uncooked fresh vegetables ·	LOW: 9
4–5-pound boned and tied piece or chunks ·	LOW: 9–10
1-inch chunks with uncooked fresh vegetables ·	LOW: 10
CROCK-ROASTED	
3½–4-pound boneless piece ·	HIGH: 3–4
short ribs ·	HIGH: 4¾ or LOW: 9½
unbrowned 3–3½-pound piece ·	HIGH: 5 or LOW: 10
ribs ·	HIGH: 2½ then LOW: 3½
marinated 3¾–4-pound piece ·	LOW: 8–9
POACHED	
unbrowned 3–4-pound piece ·	LOW: 9–10
corned beef round or brisket ·	LOW: 15

Best cuts of beef for the crock: Chuck, brisket, flank steak, foreshank, plate (short ribs).

High or low? As a rule, dry roasted meat is juicier and more flavorful cooked on High. Meats cooked with liquid must be cooked on Low.

Timing: Cooking time for beef is not as predictable as for chicken: roasts or large cuts may differ by about 1 hour on Low or ½ hour on High—sometimes more. But unlike chicken, beef does not suffer from waiting an hour or so on Low if need be. Allow yourself leeway to be safe.

Always trim excess fat before cooking. Trimming fat from stew meat is crucial. If the butcher has wrapped a sheet of fat over a tied roast, however, you may find it easier to remove the melted fat from the juices after the meat is cooked.

❦

BRAISED BEEF

*4–5 pounds center-cut
  chuck beef with bone in
  or 3 pounds boneless
  chuck roast
2–3 tablespoons oil
1½ teaspoons salt
¼ teaspoon freshly ground
  pepper
2 large onions, chopped*

*½ green pepper, chopped
3 cloves garlic, minced
2 16-ounce cans tomatoes,
  broken up
1 small bay leaf, crumbled
3–4 tablespoons each flour
  and softened margarine
  (optional)
Chopped parsley*

If meat with bone won't fit in crock, cut out bone and tie meat into compact shape with string. Or cut into large chunks. Brown meat in oil. Sprinkle with 1 teaspoon salt and ¼ teaspoon pepper. Mix onions, green pepper, garlic, tomatoes, bay leaf and ½ teaspoon salt. Make bed of vegetables in crock, lay in meat, cover with remaining vegetables. Cover* and cook 9 to 10 hours on Low or until tender. Remove to warmed platter. Adjust seasoning. If desired, thicken juices in skillet by rubbing flour and margarine together and whisking in. Pour over meat. Sprinkle with parsley. *Makes 4 servings per pound of boneless meat, 2–3 servings per pound of meat with bone.*

❦

BEEF STEW FOR A PARTY

1 recipe Braised Beef
 (p. 80)
1 stalk celery, chopped
1 teaspoon salt
¼ cup dry red wine
1 teaspoon bottled gravy
 coloring
6 medium-small potatoes,

peeled and diced
1 20-ounce package frozen
 peas
4 cups sliced, fresh carrots
 or 1 16-ounce package
 frozen
Chopped parsley

Trim all bone and fat from the meat and cut into generous 1-inch chunks. Add celery and salt to the vegetables. Substitute wine for ¼ cup of the tomato juices and stir in gravy coloring. Layer vegetables, meat and potatoes in crock. Cover and cook for 10 hours on Low or until tender. In separate saucepans, cook peas and carrots until tender. Remove vegetables to warmed serving dish. Lift beef and potatoes into dish, mix with peas and carrots. Adjust gravy seasonings and thicken, if desired. Stir into stew. Sprinkle each serving with parsley. *Makes 12 servings.*

—— ❧ ——

ZRAZY
(POLISH BEEF STEW)

2½ pounds boneless
   chuck, cut in 1½-inch
   cubes
¼ cup oil
1 teaspoon salt or to taste
⅛ teaspoon freshly
   ground pepper
2 onions, thinly sliced

4 ounces fresh mushroom
   caps and stems
5 good-sized potatoes,
   peeled and sliced
¼ cup condensed cream of
   onion soup
½ tablespoon lemon juice
Cream cheese

Brown meat in 2 tablespoons oil. Remove and sprinkle with salt and pepper. Sauté onions in 2 tablespoons oil until softened; remove. Add a little more oil to skillet and sauté mushrooms until lightly browned. In crock, make a layer each of potatoes sprinkled lightly with salt and pepper, meat, mushrooms and onions, repeating twice. In skillet, blend soup and lemon juice with enough cream cheese to make ½ cup. Stir over low heat until smooth, then pour over top. Cover and cook about 9 hours on Low or until tender. Adjust seasoning. Turn into warmed serving dish. *Makes 7 servings.*

CHILI VERDE
(MEXICAN BEEF STEW)

2½ pounds boneless chuck, cut in 1-inch cubes
¼ cup oil
1¼ teaspoons salt
⅛ teaspoon freshly ground pepper
2 onions, chopped fine
2 cloves garlic, minced
2 14½-ounce cans stewed tomatoes, broken up
1 12-ounce can tomatillos enteros (whole green Spanish tomatoes), drained and coarsely chopped
1 4-ounce can diced mild green chilies
1 cup chopped parsley
⅓ cup lemon juice
2 teaspoons oregano
1½ teaspoons ground cumin
1 teaspoon ground coriander
⅛ teaspoon ground allspice
Cooked rice
Sour cream or plain yogurt

Brown meat in 2 tablespoons oil. Sprinkle with ¾ teaspoon salt and pepper. Turn into crock. Sauté onions and garlic in 2 tablespoons oil until softened. Blend tomatoes and juice into onions, with ½ teaspoon salt. Add tomatillos, chilies, parsley, lemon juice, oregano, cumin, coriander and allspice. Mix into beef. Cover* and cook about 7 hours on Low or until tender. Adjust seasonings. Serve over rice, dollop with sour cream. *Makes 9–10 servings.*

❦

TAHITIAN BEEF STEW

3 pounds boneless chuck,
  cut in 1-inch cubes
5 tablespoons oil
¼ cup soy sauce
⅛ teaspoon freshly ground
  pepper
¾-inch knob fresh ginger,
  peeled and minced
2 cloves garlic, minced
1¼ green peppers, cut in
  1-inch squares
2 large stalks celery, sliced
  thin
1 medium-large cucumber,
  peeled and diced

6 large scallion bulbs,
  chopped
3 firm medium-sized
  tomatoes, quartered
1 20-ounce can pineapple
  chunks, strained with
  juice reserved
1 tablespoon cider vinegar
2 tablespoons cornstarch
Cooked rice
Chutney

Brown meat in 3 tablespoons oil. Add 3 tablespoons soy sauce and pepper and stir to coat pieces. Turn into crock. Add 2 tablespoons oil to skillet and sauté ginger and garlic until golden. Add green peppers, celery, cucumber and scallions to skillet and sauté just long enough to glaze. Add to crock. Add tomatoes, pineapple, 1 tablespoon soy sauce and vinegar. Gently mix stew, pushing meat down beneath vegetables. Pour pineapple juice over it and cover.* Cook 8½–9 hours on Low, or until tender. Remove stew to warmed serving dish. Turn juices into skillet. Blend a little cooled juices with cornstarch, then whisk into skillet until thickened. Adjust seasonings. Mix back into stew. Serve with rice, and pass chutney on the side. *Makes 8–9 servings.*

❦

CHOLENT
(MEAT AND LIMA BEAN STEW)

In Orthodox Jewish homes this was the Sabbath dinner, brought to the village baker's oven before sundown Friday night. You don't have to be Orthodox—or Jewish—to appreciate the ease of preparing Cholent!

*1 cup dried small lima
  beans*
*2 pounds boneless chuck
  in 1 piece*
5 tablespoons oil
1 teaspoon salt
*½ teaspoon freshly ground
  pepper*
½ teaspoon paprika
½ teaspoon ground ginger
*2 onions, cut in ¼-inch
  slices*
1 clove garlic, minced
1 cup pearl barley
2 cups tomato juice
1 bay leaf
Chopped parsley

Soak limas overnight in water to cover by 2 inches. Next day brown meat in 2 tablespoons oil. Sprinkle all over with ⅔ teaspoon salt, ¼ teaspoon pepper, paprika and ginger; remove. Add 3 tablespoons oil to skillet and brown onions and garlic, sprinkling them with a little salt and pepper. Drain limas and mix with barley. In crock, layer half the onions, the meat, remaining onions and the beans and barley. Rinse skillet with tomato juice and 2 cups water, then pour over contents of crock. Bury bay leaf and cover.* Cook 12 hours on Low, or until beans are tender. Adjust seasonings. Turn into warmed serving dish and dust with parsley. *Makes 8 servings.*

❧

DAUBE PROVENÇALE
(BEEF STEW FROM PROVENCE)

The meat should be marinated for 12 hours or overnight before you begin to assemble this dish. Black olives or sautéed mushrooms may be added at the end, if you wish.

2 pounds boneless chuck,
cut into 1½-inch chunks
12 whole peppercorns
1 tablespoon rosemary
1 teaspoon thyme
Small bunch parsley, no
stems
½ cup olive oil
2 cups dry white wine
3 ounces salt pork, cut
into small dice
1 pound veal knuckle,
cracked by butcher
3 large onions, chopped

2 cloves garlic, minced
2 carrots, cut in 2-inch
strips
3 fresh tomatoes, coarsely
chopped
2 teaspoons salt
¼ teaspoon freshly ground
pepper
¼ cup flour
Chopped parsley
Boiled potatoes

Set beef in shallow dish. Add peppercorns, rosemary, thyme, parsley, ⅓ cup olive oil and wine. Cover and set in cool place 12 hours. Sauté salt pork in ungreased skillet until golden; remove. Lift beef from marinade and pat dry. Brown in the salt pork drippings; remove. Brown veal knuckle; remove. Add 1 or 2 tablespoons oil and sauté onions and garlic until golden. In crock, make a layer each of onions, meat, carrots, tomatoes, onions, bones, and salt pork, seasoning lightly as you go. Strain marinade, pour over and cover.* Cook 8–9 hours on Low, or until tender. Remove meat and vegetables to warmed serving dish. Put flour into skillet, whisk in enough crock juices to make a paste, then whisk in the remaining crock juices and simmer until thickened. Adjust seasonings and pour over meat. Sprinkle with parsley. Serve with boiled potatoes. *Makes 5–6 servings.*

❦

GREEN PEPPER STEAK

1⅓ pounds skirt steak
¼ cup oil
3 large green and/or sweet
   red peppers, thinly sliced
3 large onions, thinly sliced
3 large ripe tomatoes,
   thinly sliced

2 teaspoons salt
Freshly ground pepper
1 16-ounce can beef gravy
1 8-ounce can tomato sauce
1½ teaspoons basil
Cooked rice

Cut meat on the bias in inch-thick strips and pat dry. Brown meat in 2 tablespoons oil until no longer pink; remove. Add more oil to skillet and lightly brown peppers and onions. Mix in meat, tomatoes, salt and pepper. Turn into crock. Blend gravy, tomato sauce and basil together. Put in crock and stir gently to blend. Cover* and cook 2½ hours on High or 5 hours on Low, until meat is tender. Adjust seasonings. Serve over rice. *Makes 4 servings.*

❦

FLEMISH BEEF IN BEER

Rye bread crumbs give flavor and body to this dish. Serve it with beer.

1½ pounds flank or skirt
   steak, cut in thin strips, 3
   inches long
3 tablespoons butter or
   margarine
1 teaspoon salt
Freshly ground pepper
2 onions, coarsely chopped
1 tablespoon dark brown
   sugar
1 tablespoon red-wine
   vinegar or cider vinegar

1 tablespoon Dijon
   mustard
½ teaspoon thyme
1 bay leaf
½ cup firmly packed stale
   rye bread crumbs
1 12-ounce bottle beer
2 tablespoons each softened
   margarine and flour
Chopped parsley

Brown meat in 2 tablespoons margarine; remove. Sprinkle with salt and pepper. Add 1 tablespoon margarine and lightly brown onions in skillet. Add brown sugar and sauté a few seconds, then stir in vinegar and turn off heat. Blend in mustard, thyme and crumbled bay leaf. In crock make a layer each of onions, meat and bread crumbs, repeating once. Pour beer over all and cover.* Cook 5 to 5½ hours on Low, or until meat is tender. Remove meat and onions to warmed serving dish. Put juices in skillet. Rub margarine into flour and whisk into juices until thickened. Adjust seasonings. Pour over meat and garnish with parsley. *Makes 5–6 servings.*

❧

STUFFED BEEF BIRDS

2½ pounds beef cube steak
1 4-ounce can mushrooms,
    drained
2 scallions
1 small stalk celery,
    including leaves
1 clove garlic
½ cup uncooked rice
2 tablespoons oil
Scant ¼ teaspoon salt
⅛ teaspoon freshly ground
    pepper

2 tablespoons butter or
    margarine
1 15-ounce can beef gravy
1 10¾-ounce can con-
    densed tomato soup
¼ cup Madeira
1½ teaspoons bottled gravy
    coloring
Chopped parsley

Cut meat into 8 pieces of equal size. Pound each piece between 2 sheets of wax paper as thin as possible. Cut and and fit pieces by overlapping and then pounding together until all are a uniform 7 by 7 inches. Chop mushrooms with scallions, celery and garlic until very fine. Sauté rice in oil until clear. Add vegetables, salt and pepper. Mix well and sauté 2 to 3 minutes more. Divide filling among meat pieces, placing filling at one end. Fold over each side to cover filling and roll up. Tie securely but not too tight with string in 3 places. Brown birds in margarine so that any tears will seal. Mix gravy, tomato soup, Madeira and gravy coloring to make gravy. Moisten bottom of crock with gravy. Arrange birds in 3 layers, moistening with gravy. Add any remaining gravy to crock and cover.* Cook 15 minutes on High, then turn to Low for another 5¾ to 6 hours, or until meat is tender. Adjust seasonings. Remove to warmed serving dish and sprinkle with parsley. *Makes 8 servings.*

MUSHROOM-STUFFED FLANK STEAK

Serve this with buttered noodles and braised carrots.

1½–1¾ pounds flank steak
1-ounce packet onion-
mushroom soup mix
¾ teaspoon thyme
½ cup chopped parsley
½ teaspoon freshly ground
pepper or to taste
6 ounces small mushrooms
or 1 4-ounce can, drained
6 tablespoons olive oil
4 carrots, cut in matchstick-
sized strips

2 stalks celery, cut in
matchstick-sized strips
1 onion, sliced thin
1 clove garlic, minced
1 teaspoon salt
Dash of ground ginger
3 tablespoons Madeira
1 teaspoon lemon juice
1 8-ounce can tomato sauce
1 teaspoon bottled gravy
coloring
Parsley

Lay meat on waxed paper. Mix soup mix, ½ teaspoon thyme, ¼ cup chopped parsley and ¼ teaspoon pepper and press into both sides. Pat mushrooms dry and brown lightly in 1 tablespoon oil; remove. Add 3 to 4 more tablespoons oil to skillet and lightly brown carrots, celery, onion and garlic. Mix in ¼ teaspoon thyme, ¼ cup parsley, ¼ teaspoon pepper, salt, ginger, 1 tablespoon Madeira and lemon juice; remove. Trim meat into an even rectangle, saving trimmings. Heap mushrooms at one narrow end, roll up tight, overlapping about 2 inches at end. Tie securely with string in several places along roll. Tuck meat trimmings into ends and tie firmly lengthwise to close openings. Add a little more oil to skillet and brown roll all over. Blend tomato sauce, 2 tablespoons Madeira and gravy coloring. Put a third of the vegetables in crock, add meat roll and arrange remaining vegetables around and over meat. Pour sauce over all and cover.* Cook 8½ hours on Low, or until tender. Set meat on warmed serving platter, arrange vegetables around it. Adjust seasonings, then turn juices into warmed serving bowl. Garnish with parsley. To serve, slice 1-inch thick. *Makes 4–5 generous servings.*

NOTE: You can refrigerate cooked dish until the next day, then heat everything up on Low for 2 to 2½ hours, or until hot.

THAI SWEET AND SOUR BEEF RIBS

4½–5 pounds meaty beef ribs
2 cloves garlic, minced
¼ cup sugar or part honey
¼ cup soy sauce

¼ cup cider vinegar, sweet sherry, or sweet sake
½ teaspoon ground ginger
⅛ teaspoon freshly ground pepper

Trim excess fat from ribs. Blend remaining ingredients and brush all over ribs. Stack crosswise in crock, meaty sides up, moistening with remaining sauce. Cover* and cook 2½ hours on High, then turn to Low and cook 3½ hours more. Lift ribs onto warmed serving dish. Put juices in skillet and boil until thick. Adjust seasonings, then pour back over ribs. *Makes 4–5 servings.*

❦
SHORT RIBS AND POTATOES

4 pounds lean meaty beef
   short ribs
1 tablespoon oil
1 large onion, chopped
1 clove garlic, minced
6 tomatoes, peeled and
   chopped
1 4-ounce can mushroom
   stems and pieces, drained
2 teaspoons dill
1 tablespoon Worcester-
   shire sauce

1½ teaspoons salt
½ teaspoon pepper
6 medium-sized potatoes,
   peeled, halved and sliced
   ¼ inch thick
3 tablespoons flour
¼ cup sour cream or thick
   plain yogurt
Chopped parsley

Brown ribs in oil; remove. Lightly brown onion and garlic in skillet. Add tomatoes, mushrooms, dill, Worcestershire, salt and pepper. Toss one-third of this mixture with potatoes and place in crock. Layer ribs and remaining sauce in crock, ending with sauce. Cover and cook about 4¾ hours on High or 9½ hours on Low, until tender. Remove ribs and potatoes to warmed serving dish. Blend flour and sour cream in skillet. Remove fat, then whisk in juices until thickened. Adjust seasoning. Pour over dish and dust with parsley. *Makes 6 servings.*

❦

POT ROAST PAPRIKA

2 large onions, chopped
3 cloves garlic, minced
2 tablespoons oil
1 tablespoon paprika
1 teaspoon caraway seeds
5 to 6 potatoes, peeled,
　quartered, then cut in
　¼-inch slices
2 teaspoons salt
3–3½ pounds boneless
　chuck or brisket
½ teaspoon freshly ground
　pepper

4 tomatoes or 1 14½-ounce
　can stewed tomatoes,
　drained and chopped
3 tablespoons dry red wine
　or vermouth
1 teaspoon bottled gravy
　coloring
2 tablespoons flour
¼ cup sour cream or plain
　yogurt

Lightly brown onions and garlic in oil. Stir in paprika and caraway seeds and sauté until seeds pop. Sprinkle potatoes with 1 teaspoon salt. Sprinkle meat with 1 teaspoon salt and the pepper. Spread one-third onions on bottom of crock. Add one-third potatoes. Set in meat. Tuck remaining potatoes around and near sides. Spread tomatoes over top. Rinse skillet with wine and stir in gravy coloring. Pour over contents of crock. Cover and cook 10 hours on Low, or until tender. Remove meat and vegetables to warmed serving dish. Mix flour and sour cream in skillet. Remove fat from juices and whisk into skillet until thickened. Adjust seasonings. Slice meat and pour gravy over it. *Makes 8 servings*

❧

CROCK-ROASTED BEEF

3½–4 pounds boneless
   chuck roast
2 tablespoons oil
1 onion, finely chopped
2 cloves garlic, minced
2 teaspoons bottled gravy
   coloring
½ teaspoon salt or to taste

⅛ teaspoon freshly ground
   pepper or to taste
2 carrots, sliced lengthwise
¼ cup dry red wine
   (optional)
¼ teaspoon dill (optional)
About 2 tablespoons corn-
   starch (optional)

Leave added fat wrapped around meat, if any. Brown meat in ungreased skillet; remove. Add oil and brown onion and garlic; remove. Add gravy coloring to skillet, roll meat in it until thoroughly covered. Sprinkle with salt and pepper. Put half of onions in crock and add meat. Cover with remaining onions. Scrape skillet juices over all. Slip carrot slices between meat and crock walls every inch or so. Cook 3 to 4 hours on High, or until tender. Do not overcook. Let meat set 10 minutes, then slice very thin, removing fat. Remove fat from juices and adjust seasonings. Serve beef in juices or blend wine, dill and cornstarch and whisk into juices until thickened. *Makes 3–4 servings per pound.*

❧

BEEF IN CREAM

1 recipe Crock-Roasted Beef
2 cups heavy cream

½ cup defatted crock juices
Chopped parsley

Keep thinly sliced meat hot. Simmer cream in large skillet, reducing it to 1 cup. Stir in crock juices, taste for seasoning and ladle over meat. Serve dusted with parsley. Good with broad egg noodles.

❦

A CLASSIC SAUERBRATEN
(GERMAN POT ROAST)

Allow 5 days for this pot roast to marinate before you cook it. It's good with potato pancakes or noodle pudding.

*3¾–4 pounds shoulder
    or other boneless chuck
    beef roast, trimmed
1 large onion, thinly sliced
1 large stalk celery, thinly
    sliced
1 large carrot, thinly sliced
24 allspice berries
12 peppercorns
2½ cups cider vinegar
¼ cup oil
1 teaspoon salt
¼ teaspoon freshly ground
    pepper*

*12 gingersnaps, crushed
1 10½-ounce can of beef
    gravy
½ cup claret or other dry
    red wine
½ cup melted red currant
    jelly or sour cherry
    preserves
3 tablespoons dark brown
    sugar
2½ tablespoons lemon juice
2 tablespoons tomato paste
1 teaspoon Worcestershire
    sauce*

Set meat in deep bowl and cover with onion, celery, carrot, allspice berries, peppercorns, vinegar and 2½ cups water. Cover and refrigerate 5 days. Lift meat from marinade, returning any vegetables to bowl. Pat meat thoroughly dry and brown in 2 tablespoons oil. Sprinkle with salt and pepper and set in crock. Strain vegetables so marinade goes into another skillet or pot. Pat vegetables thoroughly dry and lightly brown in meat skillet in 2 tablespoons oil. Add to crock. Reduce marinade to 2½ cups. Add gingersnaps, beef gravy, wine, jelly, brown sugar, lemon juice, tomato paste and Worcestershire to marinade and heat, stirring. Pour over contents of crock. Cover and cook 8 to 9 hours on Low, or until tender. Remove meat to warmed platter. Purée sauce in food mill or blender. Adjust seasoning, particularly the sour-sweet balance, adding vinegar or dark brown sugar if needed. Slice meat and pour sauce over it. *Makes 10 servings.*

❦

BASIC BOILED BEEF

Not boiled at all, but gently poached.

2 tomatoes, peeled and
  chopped
1 large onion, chopped
2 large carrots, thinly
  sliced
1 large stalk celery with
  leaves, thinly sliced
1 small turnip, peeled and
  diced
Small bunch parsley, no
  stems, chopped
2 large cloves garlic,
  minced

¼ teaspoon freshly ground
  pepper
1 bay leaf, crumbled
2¾ pounds round,
  shoulder or chuck roast,
  tied to fit crock
4 cups beef broth
1 teaspoon salt or to taste
½ cup soup pasta, cooked
  (optional)
Chopped parsley

Mix tomatoes, onion, carrots, celery, turnip, parsley, garlic, pepper and bay leaf. Put half into crock, add meat, then cover with remaining mixture. Pour broth over all, shaking crock to mix ingredients. Add salt. Cover and cook 9 to 10 hours on Low, or until tender. Remove meat to warmed serving platter. Place vegetables around it and keep warm. Serve the broth as a first course, adjusting seasonings and adding soup pasta, if you like. Or serve sliced beef and vegetables in the broth in large soup bowls. Dust with parsley. *Makes 8–9 servings.*

This meat is good with wedges of buttered cabbage, slices of coarse dark bread, horseradish, sharp mustard, pickles and cold beer.

DEVILED CORNED BRISKET OF BEEF

*Corned brisket of beef, up
  to 4 pounds, in one piece
1 onion, sliced
1 clove garlic, crushed
3–4 cloves*

*8–12 peppercorns
1 bay leaf
Dijon mustard
Brown sugar*

Place corned beef in crock and add water to cover. Add onion, garlic, cloves, peppercorns and bay leaf. Cover, and cook about 15 hours on Low, or until quite tender. Unplug crock. Cool meat in broth. Remove to a loaf pan in which it just fits. Set a second loaf pan on top. Fill with 2 or 3 1-pound weights. Cover and refrigerate at least 8 hours. Lift off top pan, turn out molded corned beef onto baking dish. Spread meat lightly with mustard. Sprinkle with sugar. Heat in a 400° oven 30 minutes, watching to see sugar doesn't burn. Serve in thin slices. *Makes about 4 servings per pound.*

For IRISH CORNED BEEF AND CABBAGE, keep meat hot. Cook 4 quartered potatoes, 5 onions. 2 small cabbages in wedges, and 8 carrots, in chunks, on top of the stove in the broth. Heap around meat on platter. Serve with mustard and horseradish.

DOWN-HOME CORNED BEEF

*3 pounds corned brisket
  or round of beef, trimmed
3½ teaspoons bottled gravy
  coloring
1 cup catsup
2 tablespoons brown sugar
1 tablespoon vinegar*

*1 tablespoon Worcestershire
  sauce
1½ teaspoons spicy mustard
1 tablespoon dill
2 carrots, sliced lengthwise
1 tablespoon cornstarch*

Roll meat compactly and tie securely. Brown in ungreased skillet. Remove from heat and brush with gravy coloring. Lift into crock. In skillet, blend catsup, brown sugar, vinegar, Worcestershire sauce, mustard and dill. Pour over meat. Slip carrot slices between meat and crock walls where they touch. Cover and cook about 5½ hours on High, or until tender. Remove meat to warmed platter. Turn juices into skillet. Remove fat. Cool a little of the juices and blend into cornstarch, then whisk into juices until thickened. Adjust seasonings. Slice meat and pour sauce over it. *Makes 7–8 servings.*

Nine

PORK, LAMB AND VEAL

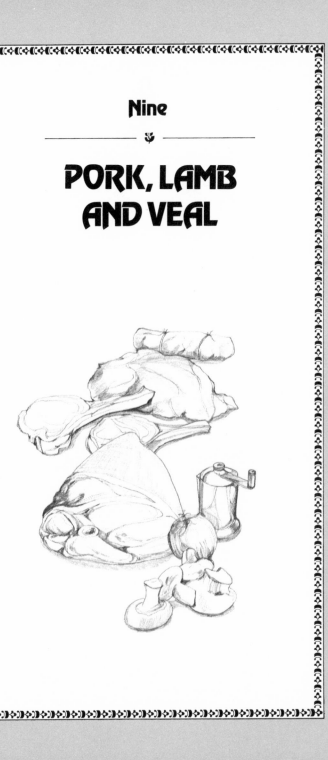

❦

COOKING PORK, LAMB AND VEAL
IN THE CROCK

PORK

Shape   *Setting/Hours*

BRAISED

¼-inch slices · Low: 7

1–2 pounds boneless piece,
depending upon other
ingredients · Low: 8–10

1-inch chunks · Low: 9

Chops · Low: 9 or HIGH: 4½

Spareribs, browned after
baking · Low: 9 or HIGH: 4½

CROCK-ROASTED

3–4 pounds roast · HIGH: 5½ or Low: 11

Cuts of pork best for the crock: Any cut of pork is successful in the crock.

High or low? Without liquid meat is tastier on High. With liquid it must be slow-simmered on Low.

Timing: Pork seems more predictable than beef, but always allow a little extra time until you've cooked enough to be certain.

Always trim excess fat before cooking.

LAMB

Shape   *Setting/Hours*

BRAISED

3–4 pounds roast · Low: 6½

Shanks · Low: 6½

Neck slices · Low: 8–8½

Shape	*Setting/Hours*

CROCK-ROASTED

3–4 pounds browned roast · HIGH: 3¼ or Low: 6½
3–4 pounds unbrowned roast · HIGH: 3½ or Low: 7

POACHED

2½–3 pounds roast · Low: 9

Cuts of lamb best for the crock: Any cut is successful. Buy the leg for a roast or company stew, meaty neck slices for a tasty family cut.

High or low? Same as for other meats.

Timing: Lamb, being young, is predictable. But always give yourself a little leeway until you're used to the cut.

Always trim excess fat before cooking.

VEAL

Shape	*Setting/Hours*

BRAISED

3–4 pounds bony cuts;
small pieces · Low: 8
large pieces · Low: 10

CROCK-ROASTED

Stuffed rolled breast · HIGH: 3 or Low: 6
Boneless rolled roast · Low: 10

POACHED

Boneless large piece · Low: 10–11
1½-inch chunks, browned · Low: 5½

Cuts of veal best for the crock: Choose as for beef (see p. 80)—everything from the forequarter. It will be less expensive, too.

High or low? Low, generally, because the meat is so delicate. But for roasted meat, use High if not for too long.

Timing: Timing veal is very tricky. Allow yourself at least 1 hour leeway on Low and ½ hour on High.

Always trim excess fat before cooking.

※

CROCKED PORK AND BEANS

*1 pound dried Great
Northern or other white
beans*
*1 pound boneless pork
shoulder in one piece*
1 onion, grated
*1 small clove garlic,
minced*
½ cup tomato paste
½ cup brown sugar

1 tablespoon molasses
2 teaspoons soy sauce
1 teaspoon dry mustard
*⅛ teaspoon freshly ground
pepper*
2 teaspoons salt
1 12-ounce bottle beer

Soak beans in water to cover overnight; drain. Brown meat
in ungreased skillet; remove. Lightly brown onion and garlic
in drippings in skillet. Blend in tomato paste, brown sugar,
molasses, soy sauce, mustard, pepper, salt and beer. In crock,
layer sauce, beans, sauce, meat, sauce, beans and sauce.
Cover* and cook 10 hours on Low, or until tender. Stir before
serving. Meat will break apart into chunks. *Makes 8 servings.*

※

PORK AND LIMAS

*1¾ pounds boneless pork
shoulder in one piece or
large chunks*
*1 green apple, peeled and
shredded*
1 large carrot, shredded
1 onion, shredded

¼ cup chopped parsley
1 teaspoon salt
*2 cups dried large lima
beans, cooked (see p. 193)*

Brown meat in ungreased skillet. Combine apple, carrot,
onion, parsley and salt. In crock, layer beans, vegetables, meat,
beans and vegetables. Cover* and cook 8 hours on Low, or
until tender. Adjust seasonings. Vegetables make a sauce over
beans. Ladle both over chunks of pork. *Makes 4 servings.*

❧

MEXICAN PORK AND BLACK BEANS

This is best when made a day ahead.

1 pound black beans,
    cooked (see p. 193)
1 pound boneless pork,
    cut in 1-inch cubes
1 teaspoon chili powder
1 teaspoon ground
    coriander
2 teaspoons salt

1 onion, chopped
1 clove garlic, minced
1 16-ounce can stewed
    tomatoes, broken up
Freshly ground pepper
Cooked rice
Chopped radishes
Fresh cilantro or parsley

Put beans in crock. Toss pork with chili powder, coriander and salt. Lightly brown onion and garlic with pork in ungreased skillet. Mix tomatoes into crock with their juice. Add meat, pepper and 2 cups water. Cover* and cook 9 hours on Low. Ladle over rice and garnish with radishes and cilantro. *Makes 8–10 servings.*

❧

PORK AND SAUERKRAUT STEW

2 strips bacon, finely
    chopped
1 large onion, finely
    chopped
2 pounds boneless pork
    shoulder, cut in 1-inch
    cubes
1½ teaspoons paprika
¼ cup dill seeds
1 teaspoon salt

½ cup tomato juice
5⅓ cups (43 ounces)
    sauerkraut
¼ cup caraway seeds
¼ teaspoon freshly ground
    pepper
1 pint sour cream
Paprika
Boiled potatoes
Sour cream

Sauté bacon and onion in skillet until onion softens. Add pork to skillet and continue until onions brown and meat is no longer pink. Add paprika, dill seeds, salt, tomato juice and ½ cup water. Turn into crock. Rinse sauerkraut in cold water and squeeze dry. Mix in caraway seeds and pepper and arrange over meat. Cover* and cook 9 hours on Low. Remove stew to warmed serving dish. Whisk ¼ cup sour cream into crock juices and adjust seasonings. Pour over stew. Dust with paprika. Serve with boiled potatoes and dollops of sour cream. *Makes 7 servings.*

BRAISED SLICES OF PORK SAVOYARD

Allow 12 to 24 hours for the meat to marinate before you cook it. Serve with buttered broad egg noodles.

1½ pounds pork, in
¼-inch slices
1 large onion, chopped
½ teaspoon thyme
1 bay leaf, crumbled
⅛ teaspoon freshly
ground pepper
About 1 cup dry red wine
2 tablespoons butter or
margarine
1 teaspoon salt

1 tablespoon flour
3 tablespoons heavy cream
1 or 2 drops gravy coloring
(optional)
Chopped parsley

Lay pork in 1-quart dish. Add onion, thyme, bay leaf, pepper and enough wine to just cover. Turn top slices over, cover and refrigerate 12 to 24 hours. Lift slices out, pat dry and brown in butter. Turn into crock, sprinkling with salt and adding all of marinade. Cover and cook 7 hours on Low. Remove slices to warmed dish. Blend flour and 2 tablespoons cream in skillet. Whisk in crock juices until thickened. If color isn't dark enough, add gravy coloring. Swirl in 1 tablespoon cream barely blending, adjust seasoning and pour over meat. Sprinkle with parsley and serve. *Makes 4–5 servings.*

❧

PEPPERY PORK CHOPS

4 potatoes, peeled and
   diced
1 onion, finely chopped
2 pounds pork loin chops
2 tablespoons oil
¼ cup white vinegar

1 4½-ounce bottle tiny hot
   vinegar peppers
⅔ cup potato water
1 teaspoon salt
1 teaspoon thyme

Pour boiling water over diced potatoes and steep 5 minutes; drain, reserving ⅔ cup water. Pat potatoes dry. Brown onion with chops in oil; remove. Pour white vinegar and vinegar from peppers into skillet. Add reserved potato water. Place potatoes on bottom of crock, sprinkle with ½ teaspoon salt. Sprinkle ½ teaspoon salt and thyme over chops and set in crock. Spread onions over chops. Add some of the peppers, according to taste. Pour vinegar mixture over all and cover.* Cook 9 hours on Low, or until tender. Serve chops garnished with potatoes, mashing them to absorb juices. *Makes 6 servings.*

❧

APPLESAUCED COUNTRY RIBS

3 pounds country-style
   spareribs
2 cups applesauce
1 2⅛-ounce packet sweet
   and sour sauce mix
1 teaspoon bottled gravy
   coloring

¼ teaspoon liquid smoke
1 tablespoon soy sauce
1 tablespoon cornstarch
Thin half-rounds of oranges

Cut ribs apart. Mix applesauce, sauce mix, gravy coloring and liquid smoke. Dip each rib in sauce. Shake off excess and stand ribs meaty ends up in crock. Pour remaining sauce over them and cover.* Cook 9 hours on Low, or until tender. Lay ribs on baking sheet. Slip beneath broiler to glaze, about 5 minutes. Pour crock juices into skillet. Spoon off fat. Mix soy sauce and cornstarch and whisk into skillet until thickened. Remove ribs to warmed platter. Pour sauce over them and garnish with orange slices. *Makes 4–6 servings.*

SUCCULENT ROAST PORK WITH YAMS

4 yams, 2 inches thick, peeled and cut in ½-inch slices
½ cup apricot-pineapple preserves
2 tablespoons frozen orange juice concentrate
1 tablespoon soy sauce
1 tablespoon gin
¼ teaspoon ground ginger
⅛ teaspoon white pepper
3½ pounds lean roasting pork

Lay yams on bottom of crock. Mix preserves, juice concentrate, soy sauce, gin, ginger and pepper and brush all over meat. Set meat on yams. Pour remaining sauce over all and cover.* Cook 5½ hours on High or about 11 hours on Low, or until meat is tender and juices run clear. Do not overcook. Remove fat from juices. Adjust seasonings. Slice meat, garnish with yams, and pour juices over all. *Makes 5–8 servings, depending on cut.*

TRADITIONAL IRISH STEW

3 medium-large onions, chopped
Small handful celery leaves, finely chopped
1 teaspoon thyme
½ bay leaf, crumbled
2¾ pounds meaty lamb
neck slices, in 2-inch chunks with bones
5 medium-large potatoes, peeled and thinly sliced
2¼ teaspoons salt
Freshly ground pepper
Chopped parsley

Mix onions and celery leaves with thyme and bay leaf. In crock layer onions with lamb and potatoes. Season lightly with salt and pepper as you go.* Add water to within 1 inch of top. Cover tightly with foil. Cover and cook 8 hours on Low, or until tender. Serve from crock sprinkled with chopped parsley. *Makes 6–7 servings.*

❦

RUMANIAN LAMB STEW

2 pounds meaty lamb neck
   slices, cut in 2-inch
   chunks with bones
1 tablespoon oil
1 stalk celery with leaves
Small bunch parsley, no
   stems
4 large whole scallions
3 cloves garlic
1 large onion
2 large ripe tomatoes,
   peeled and chopped

1 tablespoon paprika
1 teaspoon fennel seeds
1½ teaspoons salt
¼ teaspoon freshly ground
   pepper
3 or 4 new potatoes, peeled
   and cut in 1½-inch
   chunks
2 cups frozen peas

Brown meat in oil; remove. Pour 2 cups boiling water over celery, parsley, scallions and garlic. Steep 2 minutes, then drain, saving water. Add onion to vegetables and chop fine. Pour off all but thin film of fat in skillet and lightly brown vegetables. Remove from heat and blend in tomatoes, paprika, fennel seeds, salt and pepper. Place potatoes on bottom of crock. Layer vegetables and lamb over them, beginning and ending with vegetables.* Add blanching water to meat juices in skillet, stir and then pour over crock contents to barely cover meat. Cover and cook 6½ hours on Low, then turn to High, add peas, cover and cook 1 hour more. Remove fat from juices and adjust seasonings. *Makes 5–6 servings.*

❦

LAMB SHANKS CARAVANSERAI

Like most complex dishes, the flavor of this Berber-style stew will be better a day or two after making it.

3 pounds lean meaty lamb shanks, cut in half
6 tablespoons olive oil
1½ teaspoons salt
4 large onions, finely chopped
3 carrots, chopped
1 small turnip, peeled and chopped
6 ounces dried apricots, chopped
Pinch of allspice
Pinch of cinnamon
Pinch of ground cumin
Pinch of curry powder
Pinch of paprika
Pinch of ground saffron
⅛ teaspoon freshly ground pepper
¼ teaspoon thyme
1 bay leaf, crumbled
1 cup strained juice from canned tomatoes or thin tomato juice
Steamed brown rice

In large heavy skillet, brown meat in 2 tablespoons oil; remove and sprinkle with ½ teaspoon salt. Pour off fat in skillet, add ¼ cup oil and brown onions. Mix carrots, turnip and apricots into onions and add allspice, cinnamon, cumin, curry powder, paprika, saffron, pepper, thyme, bay leaf and 1 teaspoon salt. In crock, layer vegetables and meat. Blend tomato juice with 1 cup water and pour over crock contents, pushing meat beneath liquid. Cover* and cook about 6½ hours on Low or until meat falls from bone and carrots are tender. Adjust seasonings. Remove fat. Pull out bones. Cool and refrigerate, then reheat up to 3 days later. Serve with steamed brown rice. *Makes 4–5 servings.*

❧

FRENCH BRAISED LAMB

3–4 pounds lamb roast
2 tablespoons butter or
    margarine
2 cloves garlic, slivered
1 teaspoon salt
Freshly ground pepper
6 ounces bacon, diced
3 carrots, cut in thin
    2-inch strips
1 large onion, thinly sliced

12 juniper berries (optional)
½ teaspoon thyme
1 cup dry white wine
3–4 tablespoons each flour
    and softened margarine
    (optional)
Chopped parsley

Brown meat in margarine; remove. Cut meat here and there with tip of knife and insert garlic. Sprinkle with ½ teaspoon salt and a little pepper. In skillet, sauté bacon until crisp; lift out with slotted spoon and set aside. Lightly brown carrots and onion in drippings. Remove from heat and add bacon, juniper berries, thyme, ½ teaspoon salt and a little more pepper. Place a spoonful of mixture in crock, set in meat and cover with remaining mixture. Stir wine into skillet and then pour over crock contents. Cover* and cook about 6½ hours on Low, or until meat is tender. Remove meat to warmed serving platter. Remove fat from juices and adjust seasonings. Thicken if desired by rubbing margarine into flour, then whisking into juices in skillet until thickened. Garnish with parsley. *Makes 2–3½ servings per pound.*

SHOULDER OF LAMB

*1 pound eggplant, peeled,
   cut in 1-inch cubes*
*3 large tomatoes, cut in
   eighths*
1 large onion, chopped
3 cloves garlic, minced

2 teaspoons salt
1 teaspoon basil
4 pounds shoulder of lamb
Chopped parsley
Plain yogurt (optional)

Mix eggplant, tomatoes, onion, garlic, 1 teaspoon salt and basil. Arrange vegetables in crock, then set in lamb. Sprinkle with 1 teaspoon salt. Cover* and cook about 3½ hours on High, or until meat is tender. Remove to warmed serving dish. Place vegetables around meat. Pull bones from meat and carve. Taste juices and adjust seasonings, then pour over dish. Sprinkle with parsley. Pass yogurt on the side. *Makes 6–8 servings.*

CROCK-ROASTED LAMB

3–4 pounds lamb roast
2 tablespoons oil
*1 tablespoon bottled gravy
   coloring*
3 cloves garlic, minced
¼ cup red wine (optional)

2 tablespoons rosemary
½ teaspoon salt or to taste
*¼ teaspoon pepper or to
   taste*
3–4 carrots, sliced thick
Mint jelly

Brown meat in oil. Remove from heat. Add gravy coloring and roll meat all over until thoroughly covered. Sprinkle with garlic, wine, rosemary, salt and pepper. Turn into crock, scraping juices over meat. If edges touch crock walls, slip carrot slices between them every inch or so. Cover* and cook about 3¼ hours on High or about 6½ hours on Low, or until tender. Slice lamb thin or cut into chunks. Remove fat from crock juices and adjust seasonings. Pour over meat. *Makes 2–3½ servings per pound.* Serve with mint jelly.

—————————— ❦ ——————————

DILL-POACHED LAMB DINNER

2½–3 pounds boned, rolled shoulder of lamb	*1 tablespoon dill*
	1½ teaspoons salt
6 carrots, cut in ¼-inch slices	*¼ teaspoon freshly ground pepper*
6–8 medium-small potatoes, preferably red, unpeeled, in 1½-inch chunks	*1 cup dry white wine*
	1 9-ounce package frozen, frenched green beans, thawed
1 large scallion, chopped	
½ cup chopped parsley	*Mint jelly*

Place lamb in crock, then carrots over meat. Add potatoes, scallion, parsley, dill, salt and pepper. Pour wine and 3½ cups water over crock contents. Cover and cook 9 hours on Low. Add green beans to crock, pushing beneath broth. Cover and cook 1 hour more. (Or cook 1½ hours on High, then 6 hours on Low, add beans and cook 1 hour more.) Lift vegetables into warmed serving dish. Slice meat into chunks and add to dish. Serve with mint jelly. *Makes 6–7 servings.*

For DILLED FRESH PEA SOUP, use 4 cups broth left over from Dill-Poached Lamb Dinner. Bring broth to a simmer in saucepan. Break up 2 10-ounce packages frozen peas into pot. Cover and simmer until tender. Whirl in blender or food processor. Reheat only briefly (to keep bright color) and season with salt, pepper and dill. Serve dusted with more dill. *Makes 6–7 servings.* Add any diced leftovers from the lamb and vegetables and a dollop of plain yogurt, if you wish.

❦

BRAISED VEAL IN OSSO BUCO SAUCE

2 carrots, finely chopped
2 onions, finely chopped
1 large clove garlic, minced
¼ cup oil
3½–4 pounds shanks, neck,
    breast, heel, shoulder, or
    short ribs of veal
3 tablespoons margarine
Pinch each of thyme and
    basil

2 tablespoons lemon juice
1 10½-ounce can tomato
    purée
1 10½-ounce can con-
    densed beef bouillon
½ teaspoon salt or to taste
Freshly ground pepper
Cooked pasta or rice
Gremolata (see below)

Lightly brown carrots, onions and garlic in oil. In another skillet, brown veal in margarine. Mix thyme, basil, lemon juice, tomato purée, beef bouillon, salt and pepper into vegetables to make sauce. Add sauce to crock to cover bottom. Add meat. Deglaze veal skillet with remaining sauce, then add to crock and cover.* Cook about 8 hours on Low for small cuts of veal, 10 hours for one large piece. Pull out bones and cut meat into large chunks. Adjust seasonings in sauce. Serve meat and sauce over pasta or rice and sprinkle with gremolata. *Makes 6–8 servings.*

For GREMOLATA, combine 6–8 sprigs parsley, chopped, 2 cloves garlic, minced, 2–4 anchovy fillets, minced, and the grated rind of 1 lemon. *Enough for 6–8 servings.*

❧

VEAL SHANK STEW

2½ pounds veal shanks,
    cut by butcher in 1-inch
    pieces
3 tablespoons oil
1 large clove garlic,
    minced
1 large tomato, peeled and
    chopped
3 large potatoes, peeled,
    sliced and quartered

½ cup chopped parsley
Salt and pepper
½ cup dry white wine
1½ cups frozen peas
Lettuce leaves
2 tablespoons cornstarch
1 tablespoon lemon juice
1 heaping tablespoon sour
    cream

Brown veal in oil; remove. Mix garlic, tomato, potatoes and parsley. Divide meat in 2 parts, potato mixture in 3 parts. Layer in crock, beginning and ending with potato mixture and seasoning with salt and pepper lightly as you go. Add wine and cover.* Cook 7 hours on Low. Add peas on top, cover with lettuce leaves, cover and cook 1 hour more. Remove meat and vegetables (discard lettuce) to warmed serving platter. In small saucepan, blend cornstarch with lemon juice. Whisk in juices from crock and stir over medium heat until thickened. Stir in sour cream. Taste for seasoning, pour sauce over platter. *Makes 4–5 servings.*

— ❧ —

PÂTÉ-STUFFED ROLLED BREAST OF VEAL

Serve this hot or at room temperature.

1 pound boned breast of
   veal, trimmed with bones
   reserved
¼ teaspoon salt
Pinch of nutmeg
Freshly ground pepper
Pinch of ground ginger

1 5½-ounce can liver pâté
¼ cup butter or margarine
1 tablespoon lemon juice
1 tablespoon bottled gravy
   coloring
Chopped parsley
Lemon wedges

Brown veal bones in ungreased skillet, add veal trimmings, cover with 2 cups water and simmer, covered, while preparing roll. Make an even rectangle of meat by cutting straight down from narrowest end. Use trimmed meat to lay over meat and even out thickness of piece after boning. Sprinkle with salt, nutmeg, pepper and ginger. Center block of pâté at one end. Roll up tightly, allowing 1 inch on each end for shrinkage. With seam on top, sew securely together. Squeeze pâté gently to conform to roll; tuck in ends. Lightly brown in butter. Blend lemon juice and gravy coloring with skillet juices and coat veal completely with mixture. Lift roll into crock, adding skillet juices. Cover* and cook about 3 hours on High or about 6 hours on Low, or until veal is tender. Let roast rest a few moments and adjust seasoning of crock juices. Slice roll about ½ inch thick, arrange overlapping slices on warmed platter. Garnish with parsley and lemon wedges and pour juices over meat. If serving cool, chill the stock from the bones and trimmings, remove fat, then chop aspic and use as a garnish. *Makes 4–5 servings.*

❦

POACHED VEAL IN CREAMY SAUCE

*6 scallions, white part only,
  chopped
1 clove garlic, minced
1 carrot, sliced lengthwise
¼ cup oil
2 pounds boneless shoulder
  of veal, cut in 1½-inch
  chunks
½ cup chopped parsley
1 teaspoon salt
¼ teaspoon white pepper
3 tablespoons lemon juice
1 cup dry white wine*

*⅓ cup chicken broth
10 ounces fresh mushrooms,
  sliced
1 10-ounce bag frozen whole
  small onions, thawed
2 tablespoons instant flour
½ cup heavy cream
1 egg
1 egg yolk
Pinch of nutmeg
Chopped parsley
Cooked rice*

Lightly brown scallions, garlic and carrot in 2 tablespoons oil; remove. Brown veal in oil left in skillet. Mix in vegetables, parsley, salt, white pepper and lemon juice. Turn into crock and pour wine and broth over all. Cover* and cook 5½ hours on Low. Meanwhile, lightly brown mushrooms and onions in 2 tablespoons oil. Add to crock after 5½ hours, cover and cook 2 hours more or until veal is tender. Remove veal and vegetables (discard carrot) to warmed serving bowl. In saucepan over low heat, whisk flour into juices and cook until thickened. Whisk cream, egg and yolk together, then whisk into sauce. The moment it thickens, remove from heat, add nutmeg and adjust seasonings. Gently stir into stew, sprinkle with parsley and serve with rice. *Makes 6 servings.*

Ten

CHARCUTERIE, VARIETY MEATS AND MIXED MEATS

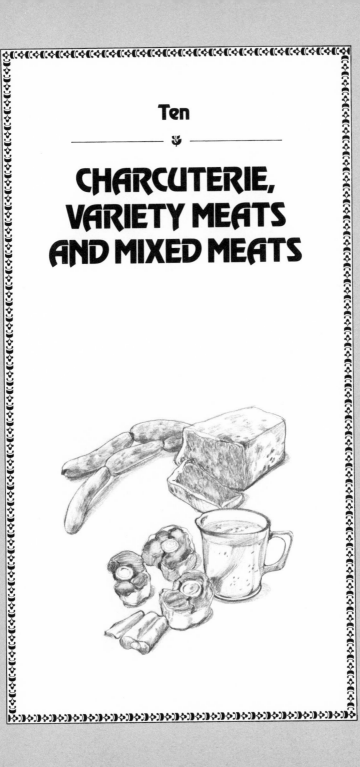

COOKING CHARCUTERIE, VARIETY MEATS AND MIXED MEATS IN THE CROCK

Shape   *Setting/Hours*

CHARCUTERIE

Pâtés and terrines, all
compositions · HIGH: 3
Ready-to-eat ham · HIGH: 1¼ or LOW: 2½
Smoked or fresh sausages · HIGH: 2

VARIETY MEATS

BRAISED

Prepared sweetbreads · HIGH: 1½
Oxtails · LOW: 7½
Kidneys · LOW: 8
1-inch chunks beef heart · LOW: 9

POACHED

Liver in large piece · LOW: 6½
Fresh tongue · LOW: 11–12

MIXED MEATS

Use temperature and time required for longest-cooking meat.

❦

LIVER PÂTÉ

1 pound chicken livers
8 thin slices lean bacon
3 large onions, finely
    chopped
½ pound sweet butter
1 cup day-old home-style
    white bread crumbs
2 eggs

Small bunch parsley, finely
    chopped
1 teaspoon salt
¼ teaspoon freshly ground
    pepper
Dash of allspice
Bay leaves
Sweet butter
Crackers or bread

Chop livers with sharp knife to confetti-sized bits, large enough to give some texture. Pour boiling water over bacon slices in bowl, set aside. Sauté onions in butter until juices have evaporated and onions are soft. Turn off heat and stir in liver until thoroughly blended. Rinse bacon with cold water, then pat dry. Lay bacon in 5-cup soufflé dish in a star shape, ends slightly overlapping in center, other ends draped over edge of dish. Mix bread crumbs, eggs, parsley, salt, pepper and allspice into liver. Turn into dish. Fold bacon over top with ends meeting in center. Lay bay leaves on top, stems touching. Set over spread-out sling (see p. 4), and lower into crock. Cover and cook 3 hours on High or until loaf pulls cleanly away from sides of dish, juices are clear and a skewer stuck in center comes out clean. Lift from crock into a larger dish. Set a plate that just fits inside soufflé dish on the meat and put a 2-pound weight on top. When meat is cold, remove weight. Pour any juices which have overflowed back into dish, cover and refrigerate until next day. Turn into serving dish. Chop up bacon with a sharp knife and blend with a fork into pâté. Lay a fresh bay leaf on each dish. To keep pâté fresh up to 4 days in the refrigerator or up to 1 week in the freezer, cover with ¼ inch of melted butter. Serve with whole-grain crackers or rough bread. *Makes 12–16 servings.*

❧

VEAL AND BACON TERRINE

16 thin strips lean bacon
4 large onions, finely
  chopped (about 2 cups)
2 large bunches parsley,
  finely chopped (about 1½
  cups)
1 teaspoon thyme
¼ teaspoon freshly ground
  pepper

1 pound veal leg round
  steak, trimmed and
  flattened
1 pound boneless chicken
  breasts, skinned and
  flattened
⅓ cup dry vermouth
1 bay leaf
Mayonnaise
Hard-cooked eggs

Pour boiling water over bacon slices in bowl; set aside. Mix onions and parsley and press out excess moisture through a sieve. Blend in thyme and pepper. Drain bacon and pat dry. Line 5-cup soufflé dish with 4 strips of bacon. Thinly layer veal and chicken in dish, beginning and ending with veal. Cover each layer with bacon and a scant 1 cup chopped onion mixture. Finish by lacing bacon over top. Pour vermouth over all and lay bay leaf on top. Set over spread-out sling (see p. 4) and lower into crock. Cover and cook 3 hours on High or until loaf pulls cleanly away from sides of dish, juices are clear and skewer stuck in center comes out clean. Lift from crock into a larger dish. Set a plate that just fits inside soufflé dish on meat. Weight it with a 2-pound weight. When meat is cold, remove weight. Pour any juices which have overflowed back into dish, cover and refrigerate until next day. Scrape fat from top, and chop any jelly beneath. Serve well chilled, sliced in wedges, with fresh mayonnaise and quartered hard-cooked eggs. *Makes 8 servings.*

—————————— ❦ ——————————

GLAZED HAM

¾ cup melted red currant   3 pounds lean boneless ham,
    jelly   in one piece
¾ cup prepared mustard   ¾ cup raisins (optional)
3 teaspoons bottled gravy
    coloring

Blend jelly, mustard and coloring. Brush all over ham. Set meat in crock, sprinkle raisins over it and cover.* Bake 2½ hours on Low or 1¼ hours on High. Remove to warmed serving platter. Slice and serve. *Makes 9–12 servings.*

—————————— ❦ ——————————

CARBONNADE OF HAM

1 onion, finely chopped   ⅛ teaspoon freshly ground
1 green pepper, finely   pepper
    chopped   4 cups (1 pound) frozen
3 cloves garlic, minced   potato nuggets
3 tablespoons oil   3½ cups (1 pound) ham, in
1 tomato, peeled and   ½-inch cubes
    chopped   ¼ cup grated Parmesan or
½ cup chopped parsley   any mild cheese
1 teaspoon thyme

Lightly brown onion, green pepper and garlic in oil. Add tomato to skillet and sauté briefly until excess juices evaporate; remove from heat. Mix in parsley, thyme and pepper. Make a layer each of unthawed potatoes, vegetables, ham and vegetables, repeating once. Sprinkle with Parmesan and cover.* Cook 1¼ hours on High or 2½ hours on Low or until hot. Serve from crock. *Makes 8 servings.*

For CARBONNADE OF LAMB, substitute cooked lamb chunks for ham, add ¼ teaspoon salt to vegetables, and sprinkle 1 tablespoon bacon bits over each layer of lamb.

❦

SAUSAGES IN WINE SAUCE

6 large mild sweet smoked
   or fresh sausages
1 large onion, finely
   chopped
1 clove garlic, minced
¼ cup butter or margarine

¼ teaspoon tarragon
⅔ cup dry white wine
1 teaspoon flour
Boiled potatoes
Chopped parsley

Brown sausages in ungreased skillet; remove and drain off fat. Lightly brown onion and garlic in margarine, sprinkling with tarragon. Add wine and stir to blend. Place sausages and sauce in crock. Cover and cook 2 hours on High. Remove sausages to warmed serving platter. Add flour to skillet, stir in a little crock juices, then whisk in remaining juices until thickened. Pour over sausages. Serve with boiled potatoes, all generously sprinkled with parsley. *Makes 3–6 servings.*

❦

KNACKWURST IN STOUT

8 (1½ pounds) knackwurst
   or other sausage

2 11-ounce bottles stout or
   other beer

Combine ingredients in crock. Cover and let steep at least 1 hour before cooking, if possible. Cook 1¾ hours on High. *Makes 4–8 servings.*

Serve this with mustard, horseradish, dill pickles, sauerkraut or boiled potatoes, if you wish.

———————— ❧ ————————

ITALIAN OXTAIL STEW

3 pounds oxtails
2 slices bacon, diced
2 tablespoons oil
2 onions, finely chopped
2 medium-sized stalks celery
    with leaves, finely chopped
1 carrot, finely chopped
1 small bunch parsley, finely
    chopped
1 clove garlic, minced
1 cup canned Italian plum
    tomatoes, drained and
    broken up

1 teaspoon salt
¼ teaspoon freshly ground
    pepper
Pinch of mace or nutmeg
1 cup dry red wine
2 tablespoons dry vermouth
1½ tablespoons cornstarch
Small macaroni or pasta
Chopped parsley

Brown oxtails with bacon in ungreased skillet; remove. Add oil and lightly brown onions, celery, carrot, parsley and garlic. Turn off heat. Mix in tomatoes, salt and pepper. Sprinkle mace over meat. Layer vegetables and oxtails in crock, beginning and ending with vegetables. Deglaze skillet with wine and pour over crock contents. Cover* and cook about 7½ hours on Low, or until meat is falling off bones. Remove meat and vegetables to warmed serving dish. Turn juices into skillet and simmer while you skim off fat. Blend vermouth and cornstarch and whisk into sauce until thickened. Taste for seasoning, then pour over stew, stirring to moisten each piece. Serve over macaroni or pasta in soup bowls. Dust with parsley. *Makes 4–6 servings.*

❦

BEEF AND KIDNEY RAGOUT

2 large onions, chopped
1 clove garlic, minced
3 tablespoons oil
2 pounds lean boneless
chuck, in 2-inch chunks
1½ pounds veal or beef
(not lamb or pork)
kidneys, trimmed and cut
in 2-inch chunks
1 tablespoon margarine
½ cup very dry sherry
(Manzanilla, if you have it)
½ cup canned condensed
beef bouillon

2 teaspoons Worcestershire
sauce
1 teaspoon bottled gravy
coloring
1 teaspoon salt
½ teaspoon freshly ground
pepper
2 tablespoons each flour
and butter or margarine
2½ cups (about 12 ounces)
baby peas (optional)
Pastry for one-crust pie
(optional)

Sauté onions and garlic in oil until golden; remove. Add beef and brown; remove. Add kidneys and margarine, if necessary, and sauté until no longer pink; discard juices. Blend sherry, bouillon, Worcestershire, gravy coloring, salt and pepper. Mix with beef and kidneys in crock. Cover and cook about 8 hours on Low or until tender. Remove meat to warmed serving dish. Rub flour and softened margarine together. Drop into crock juices in skillet and whisk until thickened. Adjust seasoning. Serve as is, or turn ragout into a baking dish and fold in thawed peas. Cover with pastry and bake in preheated 425° oven 15 minutes, reduce heat to 375° and bake 15 minutes more. *Makes 8–10 servings.*

❧

PORKALT

A tasty Hungarian stew.

3 pounds beef heart
1 quart buttermilk
1 onion, chopped
1 clove garlic, minced
5 tablespoons oil
1 teaspoon salt
1 teaspoon paprika
¼ teaspoon freshly ground
    pepper
½ teaspoon caraway seeds

1 16-ounce can tomatoes,
    drained and broken up
½ green or sweet red
    pepper, cut in thin strips
1 cup dry red wine
3 tablespoons flour
¼ cup sour cream
Cooked noodles
Chopped parsley

Cut meat in half lengthwise to lie flat; trim and cut in
1-inch cubes. Put in dish, cover with buttermilk and refrigerate, covered, overnight or up to 5 days. Drain thoroughly
and pat dry. Lightly brown onion and garlic in 3 tablespoons
oil; remove. Add meat and 1 or 2 more tablespoons oil and
sauté until lightly browned on all sides. Turn off heat. Blend
salt, paprika and pepper and stir into meat. Blend in onions
and turn into crock. Add caraway seeds to ungreased skillet
and shake over high heat until seeds pop. Turn off heat and
blend in tomatoes and pepper. Add to crock, covering meat.
Pour wine over all. Cover and cook 9 hours on Low. Remove
meat and vegetables to warmed serving dish. Place flour in
skillet and whisk in a little crock juice until smooth, then
whisk in remaining juices until thickened. Lower heat and
whisk in sour cream. Adjust seasonings and pour over stew,
stirring to moisten each piece. Serve over noodles and dust
with parsley. *Makes 6 servings.*

❧

SWEETBREADS

*1½ pounds sweetbreads,
    fresh or frozen*
Salt
Vinegar
*1 pound fresh small mush-
    rooms, with stems cut off*
*1 whole large scallion, finely
    chopped*
2 tablespoons margarine
*¾ teaspoon bottled gravy
    coloring*

*¼ cup dry vermouth or
    white wine*
¾ teaspoon salt
*⅛ teaspoon freshly ground
    pepper*
1/16 teaspoon mace
*¼ cup half-and-half or
    cream*
1 tablespoon cornstarch
Chopped parsley

Cook fresh or thawed sweetbreads as soon as possible by soaking them in cold water for about 1 hour, changing water 3 times, then placing them in pan and covering them with fresh cold water, a dash of salt and a splash of vinegar. Gently bring to boil, turn heat to low, cover and simmer 5 minutes. Drain, then plunge into cold water. Peel off membrane and separate or cut into 1-inch pieces. Lightly brown mushrooms and stems and scallion in margarine. Add sweetbreads and sauté 1 minute; turn off heat. Stir in gravy coloring, vermouth, salt, pepper and mace and turn into crock. Cover and cook 1½ hours on High or until cooked. Blend half-and-half and cornstarch and gently stir into crock. Adjust seasonings. Remove to warmed serving dish and dust with parsley. *Makes 4 servings.*

❧

POACHED CALVES' LIVER TIVOLI

This Danish way with liver is unusually delicate and creamy.

2–2¾ *pounds calves' or*
beef liver, in one piece,
trimmed
1 *large onion, thinly sliced*
1 *large carrot, thinly sliced*
lengthwise
1 *small bunch parsley, no*
stems

10 *peppercorns*
1 *bay leaf*
½ *teaspoon salt*
¼ *teaspoon thyme*
About 2 cups beef broth
Parsley

Place all ingredients except last in crock, adding enough beef broth to cover. Cover and cook 6½ hours on Low, or until center of meat is cooked but pink. Keep completely covered in broth until serving (up to 1 week in refrigerator). Slice very thin and serve hot or cool, garnished with parsley. *Makes 8–10 servings.*

You can serve the strained broth as a first course garnished with small soup pasta and a sprinkling of grated Parmesan cheese.

TONGUE À LA DIABLE

1 *onion, quartered*
1 *carrot, thinly sliced*
1 *large clove garlic, crushed*
Leaves of 1 stalk celery
1 *small bunch parsley, no*
stems

¼ *cup whole pickling spice*
6 *peppercorns*
2½–3 *pounds fresh tongue*
Splash of white or cider
vinegar
Parsley

Mix onion, carrot, garlic, celery leaves, parsley, pickling spice and peppercorns. Place half in crock, add tongue, then add remaining vegetables and spices. Sprinkle with vinegar and enough water to come to 1 inch of top. Cover and cook 11–12 hours on Low, or until tender. Turn off crock. Lift tongue out. Remove skin, fat and bones. Slice thin and return to broth in crock until ready to serve. Arrange slices on warmed serving platter. Border with parsley. Serve with Sauce à la Diable. *Makes 8 servings.*

SAUCE À LA DIABLE

¾ cup dry white wine
1 tablespoon vinegar
1 tablespoon chopped
*   scallion*
⅛ teaspoon minced garlic
⅛ teaspoon thyme
¼ bay leaf

Pinch of freshly ground
*   pepper*
1 cup canned brown gravy
1 teaspoon chopped parsley
Dash of cayenne
1 tablespoon margarine or
*   butter*

Boil down white wine, vinegar, scallion, garlic, thyme, bay and pepper until liquid measures ½ cup. Whisk in gravy and simmer 2 to 3 minutes. Strain, if desired. Stir in parsley, cayenne and margarine. Pour over meat. *Enough for 8 servings.*

CHOUCROUTE GARNIE

An Alsatian sauerkraut and meat dish.

1 pound lean, sliced bacon
1½ pounds boneless lean
*   smoked pork shoulder,*
*   cut in 1-inch chunks*
1 pound knackwurst, cut in
*   half*
1 pound uncooked Italian or
*   Polish sausages, cut in half*

3 pounds sauerkraut
8 juniper berries, crushed
2 tablespoons gin
Freshly ground pepper to
*   taste*
½ cup dry white wine
Chopped parsley
Boiled potatoes

Cover bacon strips with boiling water; set aside. Combine pork, knackwurst and sausages and set aside. Drain sauerkraut, rinse in cold water and squeeze dry. Drain bacon and pat dry. Chop bacon. Mix into sauerkraut and add juniper berries and gin. Add half of sauerkraut mixture to crock, then add mixed meats and then add remaining sauerkraut, sprinkling with pepper as you go. Pour wine over all and cover.° Cook about 2 hours on High. Turn into warmed serving bowl. Sprinkle with parsley. Serve with boiled potatoes. Pass around mustard or horseradish, if you wish. *Makes 8–10 servings.*

--- ❧ ---

CASSOULET MANQUÉ

This is not a true cassoulet because it isn't made with loin of mutton, salt breast of pork and preserved goose. But it *is* marvelous eating and freezes beautifully. Make this in advance if you can.

1½ pounds lean lamb riblets, trimmed of excess fat
1 pound chorizo or other fresh spicy *sausage, cut in 1½-inch chunks*
¾ pound bratwurst or other smoked *sausage, cut in 1½-inch chunks*
½ pound pork sausage links, cut in half
1 smoked ham hock with rind, cut in 1-inch chunks (save bone)
2 onions, chopped
2 cloves garlic, minced
3 1-pound cans or about 5 cups cooked dry butter beans or large lima beans, drained (reserve liquid)

2 1-pound cans or about 3½ cups Great Northern or cannellini beans, drained (reserve liquid)
½ cup tomato purée
⅓ cup dry white wine
Salt (see Note)
1 teaspoon freshly ground pepper
Small bunch parsley, chopped
2 teaspoons marjoram
2 teaspoons sage
Dry bread crumbs

Brown lamb in ungreased skillet; remove. Drain off fat and slowly brown sausages, stirring gently so sausage cases don't pop; remove. Carefully mix all meats together. Pour off all but a film of fat in skillet and lightly brown onions and garlic. Combine beans in mixing bowl with tomato purée and wine. In crock, layer beans and meat, sprinkling lightly with salt (see Note), pepper, parsley, marjoram and sage. Repeat 3 times, then end with beans. Tuck hock bone in center if there is room. Cover and cook 9 hours on Low. If making in advance, turn gently into bowl, cover and refrigerate. Remove all fat before reheating. If dish seems dry, moisten with reserved bean liquid. Heat gently in crock about 2½ or 3 hours on Low. Serve cassoulet in a large casserole, sprinkled with dry breadcrumbs and browned beneath the broiler. *Makes 8–9 servings.*

NOTE: Use salt sparingly in this dish; the ham hock is salty and sausages are often saltier than one thinks. Taste juices from the browned meats in the skillet to see how salty they really are, and season the layers accordingly.

— ❧ —

TAMALE PIE

This tamale pie—an old family favorite and a good party dish—can be made in stages.

1½ cups yellow cornmeal
1¼ teaspoons salt
½ cup butter or
  margarine
1 cup shredded mild cheese
2 eggs
2 teaspoons onion powder
¼ teaspoon white or freshly
  ground pepper
1 onion, finely chopped
1 clove garlic, minced
2 tablespoons oil
1½ pounds lean boneless

beef chuck, in 1-inch
  squares
1 pound lean boneless pork,
  in thin strips 1 inch long
2 tablespoons chili powder
  or to taste
½ pound lean ground beef
1 12-ounce bottle chili sauce
2 teaspoons Worcestershire
  sauce (optional)
1 6-ounce can pitted black
  olive pieces

Set crock on High. Slowly whisk cornmeal and salt into 1 quart of boiling water in crock. When smooth, cover. Cook 3 hours undisturbed. Turn into mixing bowl and beat in margarine, cheese, eggs, onion powder and pepper, one at a time. Lay waxed paper on top and set in a cool place, not the refrigerator.

Lightly brown onion and garlic in oil in large skillet. Turn off heat and stir in chuck, pork, chili powder, ground beef, chili sauce, Worcestershire sauce and olives, one at a time. Turn into crock, cover* and cook 6½ hours on Low or until tender. Turn into a buttered shallow baking dish. Spread mush down center, then with a fork smooth it evenly over top. Pie may be covered and refrigerated 1 to 2 days. Before serving, bake at 350° about 35 to 40 minutes or until bubbly. *Makes 8–9 servings.*

❦

HOCHEPOT
(FLEMISH "BOILED" DINNER)

*1¼ pounds smoked loin
pork chops, cut in 1½-
inch cubes*

*¾ pound boneless chuck
beef, cut in 1½-inch
cubes*

*¾ pound boneless stewing
lamb, cut in 1½-inch
cubes*

2–3 tablespoons margarine

*3 medium-large potatoes,
peeled, quartered, then
cut in slices ¼ inch thick*

4 carrots, thinly sliced

1 stalk celery, thinly sliced

*1 turnip, peeled, halved,
then thinly sliced*

1 onion, in ½-inch slices

*2 leeks or 8 scallion bulbs,
cut in ½-inch slices*

*1 small bunch parsley,
chopped*

1 bay leaf

2 or 3 whole cloves

1½ teaspoons salt

*¼ teaspoon freshly ground
pepper*

½ green cabbage, shredded

Brown meats in margarine. Mix with potatoes, carrots, celery, turnips, onion, leeks, parsley, bay leaf, cloves, salt and pepper. Add boiling water to 1 inch of rim. Cover and cook 9 hours on Low, or until everything is tender. About 10 minutes before finished, put a little of the cooking broth in a pot and simmer cabbage in it until tender-crisp. Turn cabbage and rest of Hochepot into warmed serving bowl. Adjust seasonings. Serve in deep bowls, with brown bread and beer, if you wish. *Makes 4–5 servings.*

Eleven

❧

POULTRY AND A LITTLE GAME

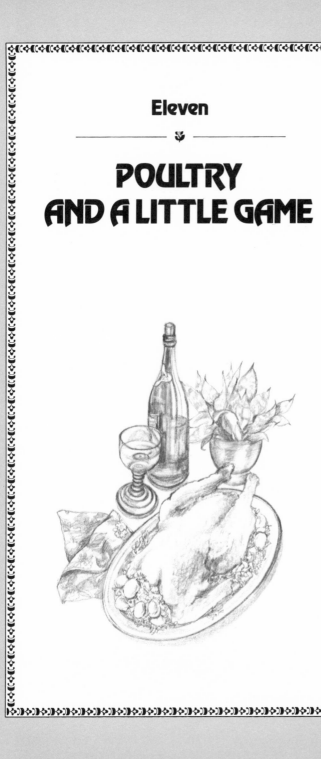

❦

COOKING POULTRY AND GAME
IN THE CROCK

CHICKEN

Shape   *Setting/Hours*

BRAISED
Chicken parts · Low: 5–5½ or High: 2¼–2¾

CROCK-ROASTED
Chicken parts · High: 2¼–2¾ or Low: 5–5½
Chicken, whole · High: 2½–3 or Low: 5–5½

POACHED
Chicken parts · Low: 5½–6
Chicken, whole · Low: 6½

UNBROWNED
Chicken parts · High: 3 or Low: 6

TURKEY

BRAISED
Large turkey parts · High: 3 or Low: 6
Wings or smaller pieces · High: 2 or Low: 4

CROCK-ROASTED
Large turkey parts · High: 3½–4 or Low: 7–8
Wings or smaller pieces · High: 2½–3 or Low: 5–6

POACHED
Turkey parts · Low: 8–9

FOIL-WRAPPED
Turkey fillets · High: 2 or Low: 4

SMALL GAME BIRDS

Shape   *Setting/Hours*

CROCK-ROASTED
Whole birds · HIGH: 1½

RABBIT

Parts · Low: 4¼–4½

———————— ❧ ————————

BASIC CHICKEN OR TURKEY, SELF-BASTED

Up to 5½ pounds chicken   *Freshly ground pepper*
  or turkey quarters or parts   *Carrot slices (optional)*
Oil   *Parsley or watercress*
About 1 teaspoon salt for
  every 3 pounds poultry

Brown poultry pieces in skillet in just enough oil to keep
from sticking. Sprinkle lightly with salt and pepper. Arrange
in crock, meatiest pieces on bottom. If cooking on High, slip
carrot slices between meat and crock, turning bony sides to
crock wall. Cover.* Cook chicken 5 or 5½ hours on Low or
2½ to 2¾ hours on High. Cook turkey 7 to 8 hours on Low or
3½ to 4 hours on High. Remove pieces to warmed serving
platter. Taste juices and adjust seasoning. Garnish with parsley
or watercress. Serve hot or cold; if cold, chill juices until
jelled, chop up and use to rim serving platter. *Allow 12 ounces
chicken or turkey per serving.*

❦

SAVORY MUSHROOM TURKEY

6–6¼ pound "fryer-
  roaster" turkey, in serving
  pieces, or up to 5½ pounds
  turkey parts
About 6 tablespoons oil
1 clove garlic
2 teaspoons salt
Carrot slices
1 packet onion or mushroom
  and beef soup mix
¼–½ cup cut-up dried
  mushrooms

1 cup beef broth
¾ cup dry vermouth or dry
  white wine
1 tablespoon each flour and
  butter or margarine per
  cup of finished broth
  (optional)
Sour cream or plain yogurt
  (optional)
Chopped dill or parsley

Brown turkey in oil, adding oil to skillet 2 tablespoons at a time. Rub crock with garlic, then drop garlic in. Sprinkle turkey with salt. Arrange pieces meaty sides down, bony sides against crock walls. Slip carrot slices between meat and walls where they touch. Sprinkle with soup mix and mushrooms as you layer. Deglaze skillet with broth and vermouth and pour over turkey. Cover* and cook about 6 hours on Low or about 3 hours on High, or until tender. Remove turkey to warmed serving platter. Pour some of the juices over the meat. Or make a thickened sauce by turning juices into skillet, rubbing margarine and flour together and whisking into juices until thickened. Whisk in a little sour cream or yogurt if you wish to make it creamy. Sprinkle turkey with dill or parsley. *Makes 10 servings.*

❋

VINTNER'S CHICKEN

3 *pounds chicken parts*
2–3 *tablespoons oil*
About 1 *teaspoon salt*
¼ *teaspoon freshly ground
 pepper*
4 *ounces mushrooms, with
 stems cut off*
2 *tablespoons butter or
 margarine*
3½–4 *ounces dry or fruity
 white wine, dry or sweet*

*vermouth, light or cream
 sherry, sweet Marsala,
 white port, brandy or other
 spirits*
3½–4 *ounces cream or half-
 and-half (optional)*
About 1½ *tablespoons flour
 (optional)*
¼ *teaspoon lemon juice
 (optional)*
Chopped parsley

Brown chicken in oil. Sprinkle with salt and pepper. Lightly brown mushrooms and stems in margarine. Layer chicken and mushrooms in crock. Deglaze skillet with wine. Pour over crock contents and cover.* Cook 2¼ to 2¾ hours on High or 5 to 5½ hours on Low, or until tender. Remove chicken to warmed serving platter. Remove fat from juices, pour over and serve. Or reduce juices in saucepan over high heat 2 to 3 minutes until consistency of thin cream. Adjust seasonings. You may thicken juices, if you wish, by blending half-and-half with flour and whisking in over low heat until thickened; add a little lemon juice to taste. Pour sauce over chicken, dust with parsley and serve. *Makes 4–5 servings.*

For RICH VINTNER'S CHICKEN add 6 finely chopped shallots to the mushrooms, use Calvados or cognac for the spirits, sprinkle 1 teaspoon tarragon over chicken in the crock, and make the sauce with heavy cream.

❦

CHUTNEY CHICKEN LEGS

3¾ pounds chicken legs *1 cup (8 ounces) chutney*
2 tablespoons oil *Cooked rice*

Brown chicken in oil. Layer chicken and chutney in crock, beginning and ending with chutney. Cover* and cook 2½ to 2¾ hours on High or 5 to 5½ hours on Low. Serve from crock with rice. Add Curry Garnishes (p. 156), if you wish. *Makes 4–5 servings.*

❦

ORANGE CURRIED CHICKEN WINGS

3¾ pounds chicken wings, *4 teaspoons curry powder or*
* tips removed* * to taste*
2 tablespoons oil *¾ cup (6 ounces) orange*
½ teaspoon salt or to taste * marmalade*
1 large tomato, peeled and *Cooked rice*
* chopped*
1 whole scallion, finely
* chopped*

Brown chicken in oil; remove. Sprinkle with salt. Pour off excess fat, add tomato and sauté until most of the liquid has evaporated. Add scallion and curry powder and stir until a paste. Remove from heat and blend in marmalade. Layer sauce and chicken in crock, beginning and ending with sauce. Cover* and cook 2½ hours on High or 5 to 5½ hours on Low. Serve from crock with rice. Add Curry Garnishes (p. 156), if you wish. *Makes 4–5 servings.*

—————————— ❦ ——————————
FIVE FLAVORS CHICKEN

This Chinese sauce may also be used with duck, pork or lamb.

3¾–4 pounds chicken parts
1¼-inch piece fresh ginger
   root, peeled and finely
   chopped, or 1½ teaspoons
   ground ginger
2 cloves garlic, minced
½ cup soy sauce

½ cup honey
3 tablespoons mirin (sweet
   sake wine), dry sherry or
   gin
2 tablespoons cornstarch
Cooked rice

Trim tips off wings and pull skin off other chicken parts. Mix ginger, garlic, soy sauce, honey and spirits. Dip each piece of chicken in sauce. Place chicken in crock and pour remaining sauce over it. Cover* and cook on Low. Wings will be ready in 5 to 5½ hours, other parts in 6 hours. On High, wings will take about 2½ hours, other parts 3 hours. Remove chicken to warmed serving dish. Pour juices into skillet. Blend cornstarch with a little of the cooled juices, then whisk into skillet. Cook over low heat until thickened. Adjust seasonings. Pour a little over chicken and pass remaining sauce in pitcher. Serve with rice. Stir-fried vegetables would be nice with this, if you wish. *Makes 5–6 servings.*

❧

CHICKEN BREASTS AND ARTICHOKES

3 pounds chicken breasts
2 tablespoons oil
1 teaspoon salt
¼ teaspoon freshly ground
pepper
1 4-ounce can mushroom
pieces, drained, or 4
ounces fresh mushrooms,
sautéed in 2 tablespoons
margarine

½ cup sweet to medium-dry
sherry
1 9-ounce package frozen
artichoke hearts
Half-and-half or cream
Chopped parsley
Cooked rice

Brown chicken in oil. Sprinkle with salt and pepper. Mix mushrooms with sherry. Break apart unthawed artichoke hearts and mix with mushrooms. Layer chicken with mushrooms and artichoke hearts in crock. Cover and cook 2¼–2¾ hours on High or 5–5½ hours on Low, or until tender. Remove chicken to warmed serving platter. Reduce juices in skillet over high heat until consistency of thin cream. Stir in a little cream and adjust seasonings. Pour over chicken. Garnish with chopped parsley. Serve with rice. *Makes 4–5 servings.*

❧

CHICKEN DIANA

3 pounds chicken parts
2 tablespoons oil
3 large potatoes, peeled and
cut in matchstick-sized
strips
1–3 cloves garlic, minced
6 tablespoons butter or
margarine
1¼ teaspoons salt or to
taste

¼ teaspoon freshly ground
pepper
2 teaspoons rosemary
½ cup dry white wine or
dry vermouth
½ cup half-and-half or
cream
About 1½ tablespoons flour
Black olives

Brown chicken in oil; remove chicken and pour off fat. Lightly brown potatoes and garlic in margarine. Layer potatoes and chicken in crock, sprinkling with salt, pepper and rosemary as you go. Pour wine over crock contents. Cover* and cook 2¼–2¾ hours on High or 5–5½ hours on Low, or until tender. Remove chicken and vegetables to warmed platter. Remove fat from juices. Turn into skillet. Blend half-and-half with flour, whisk into juices over low heat until thickened. Adjust seasonings. Pour over chicken. Garnish with black olives. Serve with broiled tomato halves, if you wish. _Makes 4–5 servings._

❧

NEAPOLITAN CHICKEN

3 pounds chicken parts
¼ cup oil
½ teaspoon salt or to taste
¼ teaspoon freshly ground
    pepper
1 large (about 1 pound)
    eggplant, unpeeled, cut
    in ½-inch dice
1 onion, chopped
1 clove garlic, minced

4 large fresh tomatoes,
    peeled and chopped, or 1
    28-ounce can tomatoes,
    broken up
1 tablespoon lemon juice or
    2 tablespoons dry ver-
    mouth
1 tablespoon sweet basil
Cooked, buttered pasta

Brown chicken in 2 tablespoons oil; remove. Sprinkle with salt and pepper. Pour fat from skillet, add 2 tablespoons oil and lightly brown eggplant; remove. Brown onion and garlic in skillet; remove from heat. Add tomatoes, cooked vegetables and lemon juice or vermouth to skillet and blend well. In crock, layer vegetables and chicken, beginning and ending with vegetables. Cover* and cook 2¼ to 2¾ hours on High or 5 to 5½ hours on Low, or until tender. Remove to warmed serving platter. Serve over buttered pasta. _Makes 4–6 servings._

VENETIAN CHICKEN CASSEROLE

3 pounds chicken parts
¼ cup oil
1½ teaspoons salt
¼ teaspoon freshly ground
    pepper
1 small onion, finely
    chopped
2 carrots, finely chopped
1 stalk celery, finely
    chopped
1 clove garlic, minced

1 10-ounce can tomatoes,
    broken up (reserve juice)
3–4 dried mushrooms, cut
    in ½-inch pieces, or 4
    ounces fresh or canned
    mushrooms, cut and
    sautéed in margarine
½ cup chopped parsley
1 teaspoon basil
½ cup dry white wine
Chopped parsley

Brown chicken in 2 tablespoons oil; remove. Sprinkle with ½ teaspoon salt and a little pepper. Pour off fat in skillet, add more oil and lightly brown onion, carrots, celery and garlic. Mix in 1 teaspoon salt and a little pepper; remove from heat. Add enough juice to tomatoes to measure 1 cup. Mix dried mushrooms, tomatoes, parsley, basil and wine into skillet. Layer vegetables and chicken in crock, ending with vegetables. Cover* and cook 2¼–2¾ hours on High or 5–5½ hours on Low, or until tender. If using fresh or canned mushrooms, stir in now. Sprinkle with parsley. Serve with Polenta. *Makes about 4 servings.*

For POLENTA, slowly whisk 1¼ teaspoons salt and 1 cup yellow cornmeal into 1 quart boiling water. Cook over medium heat 20 minutes (30 in a double boiler), stirring frequently. Turn into bowl. To serve, ladle about ½ inch thick on heated dinner plates, then place chicken over it and cover with sauce. *Makes 6 servings.*

❧

CHICKEN CHANTECLAIR

Start this New Oreans dish a day ahead, so there is time for the chicken to marinate.

1 carrot, finely chopped
1 small stalk celery, leaves included, finely chopped
2 whole scallions, finely chopped
2 cloves garlic, minced
3 pounds chicken parts
About 1½ cups claret or Burgundy
2 tablespoons oil
4 slices bacon, very thinly sliced

3 tablespoons butter or margarine
3 or 4 medium-sized dried mushrooms, in ½-inch pieces
2 tablespoons red currant jelly
1 tablespoon cornstarch
Chopped parsley
Cooked buttered egg noodles

Mix carrot, celery, scallions and garlic. Place chicken in single layer in a deep dish and sprinkle with the vegetables. Add enough wine to cover. Cover and refrigerate 8 to 24 hours. Lift chicken onto paper towels and pat dry; brown in oil and remove. Strain vegetables, saving wine; pat vegetables dry. Lightly brown vegetables and bacon in butter. Add mushrooms and wine to skillet and bring to a simmer, stirring constantly. Layer chicken and sauce in crock, pour remaining sauce over top. Cover* and cook about 5½ hours on Low, or until tender. Remove chicken and vegetables to warmed serving dish. Pour sauce into skillet and boil until reduced to three-quarters of its volume. Lay paper towels on top to lift off fat. Mix jelly and cornstarch together. Whisk into sauce and cook over low heat until thickened. Adjust seasonings. Pour sauce over chicken and dust with parsley. Serve over buttered broad egg noodles. *Makes 4–6 servings.*

❧

MEXICAN CHICKEN WITH FRUIT

3–3½ *pounds chicken parts*
5 *tablespoons oil*
1 *teaspoon salt*
¼ *teaspoon freshly ground*
  pepper
1 *large onion, chopped*
2 *scallions, bulbs only,*
  chopped
¼ *cup celery leaves,*
  chopped
3–5 *cloves garlic, minced*
1 *green pepper, chopped*
1 20-*ounce can pineapple*
  chunks in natural juices,
  drained
½ *cup raisins (preferably*
  golden and dark mixed)

¼ *teaspoon ground ginger*
¼ *teaspoon ground*
  coriander
⅛ *teaspoon cinnamon*
Pinch of allspice
Dash of cayenne
1 *cup dry white wine*
1 *cup chicken broth*
3 *tablespoons cornstarch*
3 *tablespoons orange juice*
Paprika
Toasted blanched almonds
Orange slices
Avocado slices
Seedless grapes
Cucumber strips
Cooked rice

Brown chicken in 2 tablespoons oil; remove. Sprinkle with salt and pepper. Pour off fat, add a little more oil and lightly brown onion, scallions, celery leaves, garlic and green pepper. Remove from heat. Add pineapple to skillet with raisins, ginger, coriander, cinnamon, allspice and cayenne. Layer chicken and vegetables in crock, beginning and ending with vegetables. Mix wine and broth and pour over crock contents. Cover* and cook 5–5½ hours on Low, or until tender. Remove chicken and vegetables to warmed serving bowl. Blend cornstarch with orange juice. Whisk into juices in skillet and cook over low heat until thickened. Adjust seasonings. Pour over chicken. Dust with paprika. Pass around almonds, orange slices, avocado slices, grapes and cucumber strips for garnish. Serve with rice. *Makes 6–8 servings.*

❧

ARROZ CON POLLO

Pinch of saffron	3 firm tomatoes, peeled and
½ cup chicken broth	chopped
3 pounds chicken parts	½ cup chopped pimiento
¼ cup olive oil	1 cup frozen peas, thawed
1½ teaspoons salt	½ cup shrimp, cleaned
¼ teaspoon freshly ground	½ cup coarsely chopped
pepper	ham
1 small onion, finely chopped	½ cup sliced lean sausage
1 clove garlic, minced	Paprika
1 cup rice	Chopped parsley

Steep saffron in chicken broth. Brown chicken in 2 table-spoons oil; remove and sprinkle lightly with salt and pepper. Sauté onion and garlic in 2 tablespoons oil until golden. Stir in rice and sauté 1 to 2 more minutes. Mix tomatoes into skillet with pimiento and broth. Make a bed of rice mixture on bottom of crock, then layer remaining rice with chicken, ending with chicken. Lay a sheet of parchment or buttered brown paper on chicken. Mix peas and shrimp with ham and sausage and arrange on paper. Cover and cook about 2 hours on High, or until chicken is tender. Stir top ingredients once. Turn into heated serving dish, mixing gently but thoroughly. Sprinkle with paprika and parsley. *Makes 4-5 servings.*

---- ❦ ----

ROASTED CHICKEN IN THE CROCK

3–5½-pound whole chicken
2 tablespoons oil
1 clove garlic
Salt
White or freshly ground
  pepper
Onion powder
1 teaspoon thyme, marjoram,
  tarragon or basil

2 tablespoons butter or
  margarine
Carrot slices
6 tablespoons lemon juice,
  dry vermouth or dry white
  wine
Bunch of parsley

Use a cleaver to remove knobs on drumsticks. Remove tail, wing tips and all visible fat. Brown chicken all over in oil. Rub crock with garlic, drop clove in. Lightly butter. Sprinkle chicken lightly inside and out with salt, pepper and onion powder. Sprinkle herb inside and drop in lump of butter. Truss chicken to make it compact. Set in crock breast down. Slip carrot slices between meat and wall where they touch. Add lemon juice. Cover* and cook 2½–3 hours on High, or until tender. Lift chicken to warmed serving platter, pour juices over, stuff vent with parsley and serve. *Allow 12 ounces per serving.*

For DANISH STUFFED CHICKEN, sauté equal amounts of peeled apple slices and coarsely chopped onions in butter until golden. Add an equal amount of stewed pitted prunes. Season stuffing lightly with salt and white pepper. Stuff cavity.

---- ❦ ----

ROCK CORNISH GAME HENS
OR OTHER SMALL GAME BIRDS IN THE CROCK

The moist atmosphere of the crock is ideal for small game birds because they often tend to be tough and on the dry side.

1–3 1-pound domestic or wild game birds	¼ cup Madeira
5–6 tablespoons butter or margarine	Carrot slices
Salt	1–2 tablespoons red currant or other tart jelly, or any marmalade
White pepper	Bottled gravy coloring to taste
Onion powder	
Marjoram	Parsley

Use a cleaver to remove knobs on drumsticks. Remove tails, wing tips and all visible fat. Brown birds all over in a little butter. Lightly butter crock. Sprinkle birds lightly inside and out with salt, pepper and onion powder. Sprinkle marjoram inside and drop 1 tablespoon butter in each. Tuck liver in cavity, if desired. Truss birds. Stand small birds on their shoulders, backs to crock walls. Pour Madeira over them. Slip carrot slices between meat and walls where they touch. Arrange larger birds in crock as with chicken. Cover and cook 1-pound Rock Cornish game hens about 1½ hours on High, or until tender. Larger domestic birds and wild birds might take longer. Lift birds to warmed serving platter. Remove fat from juices, stir jelly and gravy coloring in. Stuff vents with parsley, pour juices over birds and serve. *Allow 1 small bird per person.*

Wild rice, puréed chestnuts and Brussels sprouts go well with the robut flavor of wild birds.

For GLAZED GAME BIRDS, use 1 teaspoon plain gelatin for every 3 tablespoons sauce. Arrange roasted birds, either whole or in serving portions, on platter. Cover and refrigerate until cold. In heatproof bowl, blend gelatin into cooled sauce made as above. Let steep 5 minutes, then set in pan of simmering water 5 minutes, until gelatin dissolves. Refrigerate until syrupy. Stir, then spoon over birds to make a light but complete glaze. Decorate with parsley and set in a cool place (not the refrigerator) until serving.

❦

POULET À LA CRÈME
(WHOLE POACHED CHICKEN
IN A CREAMY SAUCE)

3–4½ pound whole chicken
2 carrots, cut in matchstick-
   sized strips
1 small turnip, peeled and
   cut in matchstick-sized
   strips
1 leek, tender stalks in-
   cluded, or 4 whole
   scallions, thinly sliced
1 clove garlic, minced
Small bunch parsley,
   chopped
Good pinch of thyme
½ bay leaf
2 teaspoons salt

¼ teaspoon freshly ground
   pepper
About 3½ cups chicken or
   veal broth
2 tablespoons butter or
   margarine
2 tablespoons flour
1 cup poaching broth
1 cup rich milk or half-and-
   half
1 egg
2 teaspoons lemon juice
Dash of mace or nutmeg
Parsley
Cooked rice

Use a cleaver to remove knobs on drumsticks; also remove tail, wing tips and all visible fat. Truss chicken. Place chicken breast down in crock, sprinkle vegetables, herbs and seasonings around it. Add broth to come to ½ inch of top. Cover and cook 6½ hours on Low, or until tender. Remove chicken to warmed platter. Reserve 1 cup broth for sauce. Remove fat from remaining broth, turn with vegetables into warmed tureen to serve as soup. Or strain and refrigerate for another time. To make sauce, rub softened margarine into flour. Drop into reserved broth in skillet and whisk over low heat until thickened. Stir in milk. Beat egg and lemon juice together in small bowl. Beat in a little hot sauce, then whisk back into saucepan over low heat. Stir briefly (do not let simmer) and remove from heat. Add mace. Stir and adjust seasonings. Pour a little sauce over chicken and pass remaining sauce in a bowl. Garnish platter with parsley. If not used in broth, arrange cooked vegetables around the chicken as garnish. Serve with rice. *Allow about ¾ pound per serving.*

---------------- ❦ ----------------

FLEMISH CHICKEN FRICASSEE

3¾–4 pounds chicken parts
2 tablespoons oil
2–3 tablespoons butter or
margarine
1½ teaspoons salt or to taste
Freshly ground pepper
1 onion, finely chopped
1 clove garlic, minced
4 carrots, cut in matchstick-
sized strips
3 stalks celery, cut in match-
stick-sized strips
3 leeks or 12 scallions, white
part only, thinly sliced

1 small bunch parsley,
chopped
½ bay leaf
⅛ teaspoon thyme
4 cups chicken broth
4 ounces mushrooms, with
stems cut off
6–7 tablespoons each flour
and margarine, or 3 table-
spoons flour, 3 egg yolks
and 3 tablespoons heavy
cream
Parsley
Cooked rice

Brown chicken in oil and 1 tablespoon margarine; remove. Sprinkle with 1 teaspoon salt and pepper. Drain off fat in skillet and add a little more margarine. Sauté onion, garlic, carrots, celery and leeks over high heat about 2 minutes without letting them color. Mix in parsley, bay leaf, thyme, ½ teaspoon salt and a little pepper. Layer chicken and vegetables, beginning and ending with vegetables. Pour broth over all. Cover and cook 5½–6 hours on Low, or until chicken is tender. Add mushrooms and stems after about 4 hours. Lift chicken and vegetables into warmed serving dish. Pour juices into skillet. Blend flour and softened margarine together. Drop into juices and whisk over low heat until thickened. Or thicken juices with 3 tablespoons flour, whisk a little hot sauce into yolks in bowl, then return mixture to sauce over medium-low heat, stirring just until sauce coats spoon. Off heat stir in cream and adjust seasonings. Moisten chicken with a little sauce and pass the rest in sauceboat. Garnish with parsley. Serve over rice. *Makes 5–6 servings.*

For COQ À LA BIÈRE, another Flemish dish, omit celery, onion and garlic, use only 1 carrot and 1 leek, and substitute 2 cups beer for 2 cups of the chicken broth. Use twice as many mushrooms, if desired.

❦

TURKEY PICNIC ROLLS

2¼ pounds turkey breast	Basil
Freshly ground pepper	14 ounces mortadella or
Lemon juice	other lean salami, in 30
Garlic powder	paper-thin slices

Remove skin and bones from turkey. Slice ¼ inch thick. Butterfly small unevenly shaped pieces and trim or overlap as necessary to resemble fillets of sole. You should have 10 fillets. Lightly sprinkle turkey on one side with pepper, lemon juice, garlic powder and basil. Overlap 3 slices salami to fit each fillet. Lay turkey seasoned side up over salami. Roll up, seasoning in, salami out. Cut foil into 10 pieces, 6 by 7½ inches. Roll each turkey roll tightly in foil, turn up ends and twist to seal. Chill 8 to 24 hours. Arrange in crock seam sides up. Cover and cook 4 hours on Low. Serve cool, unwrapped just before serving. *Makes 10 rolls; allow 1 or 2 per serving.*

NOTE: Other ideas for rolling up with turkey might be: boiled ham or Canadian bacon, with chutney in center; dried beef, with capers in center; tongue with Dijon mustard spread on it; veal, pounded paper thin, with pâté in center. Use your imagination for more ideas!

❧

CHICKEN, TURKEY AND OTHER POULTRY PRE-COOKED FOR CASSEROLES, SANDWICHES AND OTHER PURPOSES

Undercook slightly when delicate meat is to be cooked more than once.

Up to 6 pounds poultry   *Freshly ground pepper*
Salt   *Carrots, sliced lengthwise*

Cut poultry into quarters or parts. Use a cleaver to remove knobs on drumsticks; also remove tails, wing tips and all visible fat. Sprinkle lightly with salt and pepper. Butter crock. Arrange pieces meaty sides down, bony sides and parts against crock walls. If cooking on High, wedge carrots between meat and wall. Cover, cook chicken for about 3 hours on High or about 6 hours on Low—less time if crock is not completely full. Cook turkey about 5 hours on High or about 10 hours on Low, and also for less time if not full. *Roughly allow about 12 ounces unboned poultry for every cup of pure cooked meat.*

You will have a bonus of up to 2½ cups pure broth. To glean every drop, pull skin and bones from poultry, return to crock and cover with water. Cover and cook about 6 hours on High. You will have up to 6½ cups of excellent concentrated broth.

❧

TETRAZZINI WITH ARTICHOKE HEARTS

About 10 ounces spaghetti   *1 10-ounce package frozen*
*   or other pasta*   *   artichoke hearts*
2–3 cups small chunks   *Grated Parmesan cheese*
*   cooked chicken or turkey*   *Paprika (optional)*
1 recipe Mushroom Sauce
*   (p. 21)*

Cook pasta in boiling water for 3 to 4 minutes, only until it loses its raw dough look; drain. Gently fold meat into sauce. Break up unthawed artichoke hearts and fold into sauce with pasta. Turn into oiled crock. Sprinkle generously with Parmesan cheese. Cover and cook about 3 hours on Low.

Turn tetrazzini into a buttered shallow baking dish, sprinkle with more Parmesan, and paprika for color, and brown beneath a hot broiler. *Makes 6 servings.*

CURRY FOR A CROWD

7½ pounds meaty *chicken or turkey parts, three 3½ pound whole fryers, or 1 10-pound whole turkey, cooked according to recipe on p. 138*

3 large (1½ pounds) firm cooking pears or apples, peeled and finely chopped

2 tablespoons lime or lemon juice

4 large onions, finely chopped

4 cloves garlic, minced

⅓ cup oil

3¼ cups broth from cooked poultry

¼ cup butter or margarine

¼ cup curry powder or to taste

¼ teaspoon chili powder

⅛ teaspoon cinnamon

⅛ teaspoon ground coriander

⅛ teaspoon ground ginger

Pinch of ground cloves

Dash of cayenne

1 14½-ounce can sliced baby tomatoes, drained well and chopped

2½ teaspoons salt

1 10½-ounce can condensed cream of onion soup

1 cup golden raisins

3 tablespoons each mar- garine and flour

Cooked rice

Cook poultry, saving broth and discarding skin, bones and gristle. Cut meat into good-sized chunks. Cover and refrigerate while making sauce.

Mix pears with lime juice. Sauté onions and garlic in oil until softened; do not brown. Add pears and sauté 5 minutes more without browning. Stir in 3¼ cups reserved broth. Turn into crock. Add margarine to skillet. Stir in curry powder, chili powder, cinnamon, coriander, ginger, cloves and cayenne until lightly browned; remove from heat. Mix tomatoes into spices. Turn into crock and add 2 teaspoons salt and the soup and raisins. Stir, cover and cook 1 hour on High, stirring once. Rub margarine and flour together and stir in until thickened. Adjust seasonings. Sauce will keep refrigerated up to 2 days. To serve, mix poultry chunks into sauce, turn into crock, cover and heat 2½ hours on Low, then turn to High for another 1½ hours. Stir occasionally. Serve over rice with garnishes chosen from the list below. *Makes 14–16 servings.*

CURRY GARNISHES

This list of garnishes indicates the length of time that each food may be kept in the refrigerator or a cool place. Serve each in a separate dish or bowl. Choose at least three—the more, the better.

Any chutney (indefinitely; see recipe, p. 250)

Sweet fruit pickles, such as watermelon rind, peach, fig or plum (indefinitely)

Sweet vegetable pickles, such as small sweet gherkins, small onions or chilies (indefinitely)

Relishes, such as tomato, zucchini or pineapple (indefinitely)

Chopped peanuts (2 days, if toasted first)

Salted seeds, such as pumpkin or sunflower (2 days, if toasted first)

Dark raisins (indefinitely)

Chopped candied ginger (indefinitely)

Toasted or moist coconut (12 hours)

Chopped scallions (12 hours)

Chopped or thinly sliced radishes (12 hours)

Chopped green or sweet red peppers (6 hours)

Crumbled crisp bacon (6 hours; do not refrigerate)
Chopped unpeeled green or red apples (6 hours, if tossed with ascorbic acid canning powder or lemon juice)
Chopped hard-cooked eggs (2 hours)
Chopped bananas (last-minute) or packaged dried banana flakes (indefinitely)

❦

RABBIT, CREOLE STYLE

Start a day ahead to allow time for the rabbit to marinate.

1 onion, finely chopped
1 carrot, finely chopped
1 small stalk celery, finely chopped
Small bunch parsley, finely chopped
1 bay leaf, crumbled
1½ teaspoons salt
1¼ teaspoons freshly ground pepper or to taste
¼ teaspoon paprika
2¼ pounds rabbit, in serving pieces

2 cups dry white wine
1 16-ounce bag frozen small boiling onions, defrosted
⅓ cup butter or oil
1 teaspoon sugar
¼ cup (1 ounce) finely chopped ham
1 tomato, peeled and chopped
½ teaspoon nutmeg
2 tablespoons cornstarch
Chopped parsley

Mix onion, carrot, celery, parsley, bay leaf, 1 teaspoon salt, pepper and paprika in flat baking dish. Remove half of mixture. Put rabbit in dish, cover with reserved vegetables and pour wine over all. Cover and refrigerate 24 hours. Next day, pat onions dry and caramelize them in skillet in 1 tablespoon butter and sugar; remove. Pat rabbit dry, returning any vegetables to marinade. Add 2 tablespoons butter to skillet and brown meat; remove. Strain marinade, saving juices. Pat vegetables dry. Add a little more butter to skillet, add vegetables and ham and sauté until vegetables are softened and lightly browned. Blend tomato into skillet. Stir in nutmeg, ½ teaspoon salt, a little pepper and the marinade juices. Make a layer each of sauce, rabbit and onions in crock, beginning and ending with sauce. Cover* and cook 4¼–4½ hours on Low, or until tender. Remove rabbit and vegetables to warmed serving dish. Blend a little cooled juice with cornstarch. Turn remaining juices into skillet, whisk in cornstarch and cook over low heat until thickened. Adjust seasonings. Pour over meat. Dust with parsley and serve. *Makes 4 servings.*

Twelve

❧

FISH

COOKING FISH IN THE CROCK

Fish fillets cooked on Low will be done in 1½ hours. A big piece of fish will take 3 to 3½ hours on Low. Fish poached in a great deal of broth takes longer, for it takes time to heat up the broth. *And fish cooked with other ingredients must accommodate its cooking time to the time required by the accompanying rice, potatoes or custard.* In such casseroles, however, the fish is insulated from dry heat and will not suffer from extra cooking.

Fish, Shape, *Other Ingredients*	*Setting/Hours*
Fillets covered with liquid ·	Low: 1½
1–1½-inch fillets in soup ·	HIGH: 1½ or Low: 3
2–3-pound piece (bass, salmon) in broth ·	Low: 3–3½
Shellfish, small seafood added to hot broth ·	HIGH: ½
Squid ·	HIGH: ¾
¾-inch diced fillets with rice ·	HIGH: 2
Small pieces of fillets with potato nuggets ·	Low: 2½
Cooked fish in soufflé dish ·	HIGH: 1
Cooked fish in custard dish ·	HIGH: 1¾
Cooked fish with frozen or blanched vegetables ·	HIGH: 1¼–1½
Canned clams in soup ·	Low: time it takes for other ingredients

❦

QUICK FISH DISH

1 pound cod or other
  fillets, frozen or fresh
1 16-ounce can "stewed"
  tomatoes
1 cup uncooked white rice
1 9-ounce package frozen
  peas and diced carrots
1/4 cup finely chopped onions

1/2 cup dry white wine
1 teaspoon basil
1 teaspoon salt
Freshly ground pepper
2 tablespoons, butter or
  margarine
Shredded mild cheese

Cut thawed fish in 3/4-inch dice, removing any bones. Mix in crock with tomatoes, rice, peas and carrots, onion, wine, basil, salt and pepper, pushing down beneath liquid. Dot with margarine. Cover and cook 2 hours on High, or until rice is cooked and other ingredients are tender. Adjust seasonings, turn into warmed serving dish and cover with cheese. *Makes 6 servings.*

❦

TURBOT IN ONION CREAM

1 large onion, finely
  chopped
2 whole scallions, finely
  chopped
1 clove garlic, minced
2 tablespoons butter or
  margarine
1 cup cottage cheese
1 10¾-ounce can condensed
  cream of onion soup

1 tablespoon lemon juice
1/4 teaspoon dill
3 cups (12 ounces) frozen
  potato nuggets, cut in half
1¼ pounds thin fillets of
  turbot or other mild fish,
  cut in 1-by-2-inch pieces
1/4 cup grated Parmesan
  cheese
Dill

Sauté onion, scallions and garlic in margarine until golden. Blend together cottage cheese, soup, lemon juice and dill in food processor or blender. Combine with onions to make sauce. Moisten bottom of crock with sauce. Make a layer each of potatoes, fish and sauce, repeating twice. Sprinkle top with Parmesan and dust with more dill. Cover and bake 2½ hours on Low, or until tender. *Makes 4–5 servings.*

❧

ROLLED FILLETS OF SOLE CHABLIS

1½ pounds (8) fillets of sole or other delicate fish
1 bay leaf, crumbled
¼ teaspoon thyme
2 tablespoons butter or margarine
½ teaspoon salt
Freshly ground pepper to taste

1 whole scallion, finely chopped
1 clove garlic, minced
4 sprigs parsley, chopped
About 1⅔ cups chablis or other dry white wine
2 tablespoons cornstarch
1 tablespoon sour cream
1 egg yolk
Chopped parsley

Spread fillets on working surface. Sprinkle bay leaf and thyme evenly over them. Dot each fillet with 3 or 4 flecks of margarine. Lightly season with salt and pepper. Butter crock bottom. Roll up fillets and fit seam side down in crock in one layer. Sprinkle scallion, garlic and parsley over rolls. Add enough wine to cover. Cover* and cook 1½ hours on Low. Lift rolls to warmed serving dish. Pour juices into skillet. Mix cornstarch with a little cooled broth, then whisk into skillet, cooking over medium-high heat until thickened. Blend sour cream and egg yolk in small bowl, beat a little hot sauce into them, then whisk back into skillet over low heat; do not let sauce simmer. Remove from heat, adjust seasonings, add enough sauce to moisten fish. Sprinkle rolls with parsley and pass remaining sauce separately. *Makes 4 servings.*

❦

COOL GREEK FISH WITH FRESH MAYONNAISE

A lovely, lemony fish broth is a fringe benefit of this dish. Serve it as a first course for a beautifully integrated meal.

2 onions, thinly sliced
2 carrots, thinly sliced
2 tomatoes, thinly sliced
1 stalk celery with leaves, thinly sliced
Small bunch parsley, chopped
1 clove garlic, minced
½ teaspoon oregano
½ teaspoon thyme
1¼ teaspoons salt
⅛ teaspoon freshly ground pepper
2 tablespoons lemon juice
2¼ pounds moist, large-boned fish in 1 piece, skin and bones intact
Fresh mayonnaise (see below)
1 cucumber, thinly sliced
Green olives
Boiled new potatoes

Mix onions, carrots, tomatoes, celery, parsley, garlic, oregano, thyme, salt, pepper and lemon juice. Place one-third of mixture in crock. Add fish. Cover with remaining vegetables and add 4 cups of water. Cover and cook 3 to 3½ hours on Low, until fish tests tender with cooking fork. Remove fish to counter, returning any vegetables to crock. Turn to High, cover and cook 1 hour more. Skin and bone fish and reconstruct shape on serving dish. Mask with fresh mayonnaise, cover and refrigerate. When vegetables are tender-crisp, strain broth into saucepan. Cool vegetables, then arrange around fish. Cover and again refrigerate from 4 to 24 hours. To serve, edge dish with cucumber and dot with a few olives. Pass mayonnaise on the side. Serve with cool potatoes boiled in their jackets and dressed with olive oil and coarse salt. *Makes 6–8 servings.*

FRESH MAYONNAISE

1 egg
*1–2 tablespoons lemon
  juice*
½ teaspoon salt

Pinch of white pepper
*1 cup blended olive and
  salad oil*

Place egg, lemon juice, salt, pepper, and ¼ cup oil in blender or food processor. Turn on machine and at once add remaining oil in *a very thin drizzle;* turn off. Taste and add salt, if necessary. If mayonnaise is thin, add about ¼ cup more oil in same manner. This will keep refrigerated up to 10 days. *Makes 1¼–1½ cups, about 6 generous servings.*

LEMON BROTH

3 eggs
2 tablespoons lemon juice
*Simmering broth from Cool
  Greek Fish (p. 164)*

1 cup cooked rice
Dill

Beat eggs in bowl. Add lemon juice, whisking constantly. When thoroughly blended, whisk mixture back into gently simmering broth. The moment it thickens, remove from heat. Stir in rice. Soup may be served hot, but it's better cold. Stir well and serve garnished with dill. *Makes 8 servings.*

❦

COLD CREAM SOUP FROM NORMANDY

*1 stalk celery, finely
    chopped
½ small onion, finely
    chopped
1 carrot, finely chopped
Small bunch parsley, finely
    chopped
½ clove garlic, minced
6 tablespoons butter
¼ cup dry white wine
1 pound fillets of moist
    flavorful fish or a mixture*

*of fish and seafood, in
    small pieces
3 cups milk
1 tablespoon flour
1–1½ cups half-and-half or
    cream
Salt to taste
Freshly ground pepper
Consommé
Chopped chives, scallion
    stalks or parsley*

Sauté celery, onion, carrot, parsley and garlic in ¼ cup butter until softened. Add wine and simmer 5 minutes or until cooked, stirring often. Mix vegetables, fish and milk in crock. Cover and cook 1½ hours on Low, or about ¾ hour on High, or until fish is cooked. Leave crock on High and purée mixture smooth in blender or through food mill. Put back into crock. Rub 2 tablespoons softened butter with flour and whisk into soup. When thickened, stir in half-and-half until desired consistency—soup will be thicker when cold. Add salt and pepper to taste. Turn into serving bowl, cover and chill 6 to 24 hours. If chilled soup is too thick, thin with room temperature diluted consommé or more cream just before serving. Serve dusted with chopped chives. *Makes 4–6 servings.*

For a special Normandy garnish, top each bowl with one of these: poached, trimmed oysters; steamed, shelled mussels; shelled, cooked shrimps; thinly sliced sautéed mushrooms; poached shelled crayfish; or freshly made croutons fried in butter.

PORTUGUESE FISH STEW

1 onion, thinly sliced
1 large clove garlic, minced
3 tablespoons olive oil
12 ounces thick fillets of sea
   bass or other moist-fleshed
   fish, in 1-inch pieces
1 pound small fresh clams
8 ounces medium-sized raw
   unshelled shrimp (frozen
   thawed is fine)

1 14½-ounce can tomatoes
1 cup dry port wine
2 tablespoons lemon juice
1 teaspoon basil
2 teaspoons salt
¼ teaspoon freshly ground
   pepper or to taste

Lightly brown onion and garlic in 1 tablespoon oil. Mix with remaining ingredients in crock, adding 2 cups of water and drizzling remaining 2 tablespoons oil on top. Cover and cook 3 hours on Low or 1½ hours on High, or until tender. Stir gently to blend. Adjust seasonings. *Makes 4–6 servings.*

SANTA MONICA BAY BOUILLABAISSE

Make the broth one day, the soup the next. ("Bouillabaisse" has come to mean an elegant herbal fish stew, and since we can't make it with the *rascasses* and *hirondelles de la mer* we're supposed to, we made it—superbly—with fish close at hand.)

1 pound squid
4 ounces raw shrimp
Generous 1 pound large
  fish bones, chopped up
1 carrot, thinly sliced
  lengthwise
1 stalk celery with leaves
  included, thinly sliced
1 onion, thinly sliced
1 large ripe tomato, peeled
  and chopped
4 sprigs parsley, chopped
1 clove garlic, crushed
1 tablespoon basil
¼ teaspoon fennel seeds
1 teaspoon salt
¼ teaspoon freshly ground
  pepper

1 bay leaf
2 tablespoons lemon juice
½ cup olive oil
4 teaspoons chicken bouillon
  powder
2 cups dry white wine
1 bottle clam juice
3 small tomatoes, chopped
¼ teaspoon hot pepper
  sauce
⅛ teaspoon ground saffron
1¾ pounds thick fillets of
  moist-fleshed fish; 3 dif-
  ferent kinds
12 small clams or 1 10-ounce
  can whole baby clams

Clean squid under cold running water: pull tentacled body from hood; pull out and discard feather-shaped shell inside hood; press out contents of hood and rinse well; rub off speckled membrane. Wrap hoods in waxed paper and refrigerate. Trim tentacles off head and discard head. Remove shells from shrimp; set aside. Clean shrimp, wrap and refrigerate. Put bones, tentacles, shrimp shells, carrot, celery, onion, tomato, parsley and garlic into crock. Add 2 teaspoons basil, fennel seeds, salt, pepper, bay leaf, lemon juice, ¼ cup oil and 2 teaspoons chicken bouillon powder; stir well. Pour wine, clam juice and 3 cups water over all. Cover and cook 12 hours on Low or up to 15, if convenient. Pour stock through strainer, holding back the residue at the bottom. Discard contents of strainer. Measure stock; you'll need 7 cups. Simmer it down or add more white wine or water to get the right amount.

When crock has cooled, rinse out, add stock and turn to High. Add tomatoes, pepper sauce, saffron, 1 teaspoon basil, 2 teaspoons chicken bouillon powder and ¼ cup oil. Cut squid into ¼-inch rings and stir into crock. Cover and cook 15 minutes. Turn off crock and let it stand in a cool place 6 hours.

Cut fillets of fish in 1½-inch pieces. Turn crock to High and add fish, stirring to blend. Cover and cook 1 hour. Add clams and shrimp, stirring gently. Cover and cook ½ hour more. Adjust seasonings, turn into warmed tureen and serve. Or lift the fish with just enough broth to moisten into a warmed serving dish and serve as a separate course after the broth. Garlic croutons are a nice garnish if the broth is served separately. *Makes 6–8 servings.*

ROUILLE, a Provençale sauce, gives an incomparable finishing touch to the fish, whether fish is served plain or in broth. Pound together in a mortar or blend in food processor or blender 4 cloves garlic and 4 small drained, canned pimientos. Soak ½ cup bread crumbs in water, squeeze dry and blend into paste. Slowly trickle in 4–6 tablespoons olive oil. Thin to thick-sauce consistency by slowly beating in broth from bouillabaisse. Add salt and pepper to taste. Serve in a sauce dish. *Makes about 1 cup; allow 1–2 tablespoons per serving.*

---------------- ❧ ----------------

CHEESE CUSTARD FISH SUPPER

Good with leftovers; children take seconds.

1 10½-ounce can cheese sauce
3 eggs
½ teaspoon onion powder
1 generous cup flaked cooked or drained canned fish
1½ cups cooked vegetables
(mixture of sliced onions, chopped tomatoes, sliced carrots and peas, for example)
2 cups peeled cooked potato chunks or frozen potato nuggets, chopped
Dill

Set crock at High. Beat cheese sauce, eggs and onion powder to blend. Add fish, vegetables and potato chunks. Stir well and turn into buttered 5-cup soufflé dish. Set over spread-out sling (see p. 4). Dust with dill. Set in crock. Cover and bake 1¾ hours. Serve hot. *Makes 6 servings.*

❦

SALMON MOUSSE

2 tablespoons melted butter
   or margarine
2 tablespoons flour
1 16-ounce can salmon
¼ teaspoon salt
¼ teaspoon onion powder
3 eggs, separated
⅛ teaspoon white pepper

½ teaspoon dill
1 teaspoon lemon juice
1 cup heavy cream
Parsley
Capers
Alice Vinegar's Egg Sauce
   (see below)

Set crock at High 20 minutes before beginning. Butter 5-cup soufflé dish. Set over spread-out sling (see p. 4). Blend margarine and flour in large saucepan. Whisk in ¼ cup broth from salmon (discard rest), salt and onion powder. Whisk until thickened; remove from heat. Whisk flaked salmon, egg yolks, white pepper, dill and lemon juice into saucepan. Beat egg whites until stiff but not dry; reserve. Beat cream until stiff. Fold cream into fish lightly but thoroughly. Fold in whites, leaving unblended patches. Turn into dish and set in crock. Cover and bake 1 hour. Serve at once. Garnish each serving with parsley and capers. Pass sauce on the side. *Makes 4–6 servings.*

ALICE VINEGAR'S EGG SAUCE

¼ cup melted butter
¼ cup flour
1⅓–1⅔ cups half-and-half
   or rich milk

1 teaspoon white or tarragon vinegar
Salt to taste
White pepper to taste
3 hard-cooked eggs, shelled
   and cut in 6 slices each

Blend butter and flour in small saucepan. Slowly whisk in about 1⅓ cups half-and-half over medium heat. When thickened, whisk in more half-and-half until consistency of medium-thick sauce. Add vinegar. Adjust seasonings. Remove from heat and fold in eggs. Keep warm over simmering water until needed. *Makes 4–6 servings.*

❧

ITALIAN SWEET AND SOUR TUNA RAGOUT

Use any strong-flavored fresh, canned or cooked fish in this recipe.

1 large onion, chopped
2 tablespoons oil
1 large green pepper,
  cut in thin strips
1 12-ounce bag frozen
  whole small onions,
  unthawed
1 9-ounce package (2 cups)
  frozen Italian green beans,
  unthawed
2 cups canned tomatoes,
  broken up
2 teaspoons basil
½ teaspoon marjoram

1 tablespoon vinegar
1 teaspoon lemon juice
2 teaspoons sugar
1 teaspoon salt
Fresh ground pepper
5 tablespoons catsup
14–16 ounces (2 cups flaked)
  chunk-style tuna or any
  strongly flavored fresh,
  frozen, canned, or left-
  over fish
Generous 1 tablespoon
  cornstarch

Brown onion in oil in large skillet. Add green pepper and unthawed onions and sauté 2–3 minutes; remove from heat. Stir in green beans, tomatoes, basil, marjoram, vinegar, lemon juice, sugar, salt and pepper. When blended, mix in ¼ cup catsup. If using uncooked fish or thawed frozen fish, break into large flakes and distribute among vegetables in crock. Cover and cook 1¼–1½ hours on High. If using canned or cooked fish, gently mix into stew after ½ hour. To finish sauce, blend cornstarch with 1 tablespoon catsup and stir into crock. Serve from crock with lots of Italian bread for the sauce. *Makes 6 servings.*

If you wish, add blanched thin rounds of carrots to the ragout or lightly browned cubes of eggplant. A handful of black olives at the end will add dash and color.

❧

MANHATTAN CLAM CHOWDER

*4 ounces salt pork, cut in
    ½-inch dice
1 large onion, thinly sliced
4 medium-sized potatoes,
    peeled and cut in ¼-inch
    dice
½ large green pepper, cut
    in ¼-inch dice
1 stalk celery with leaves,
    cut in ¼-inch dice
Small bunch parsley,
    chopped*

*2 cups coarsely chopped
    fresh or firm canned
    tomatoes
2 8-ounce cans minced clams
½ teaspoon thyme
½ teaspoon salt
½ teaspoon freshly ground
    pepper
3 cups water*

Brown salt pork in skillet; remove bits to crock. Sauté onion in drippings until golden; add to crock. Add potatoes, green pepper, celery, parsley, tomatoes, clams, thyme, salt, pepper and water. Cover and cook 8 hours on Low. Adjust seasonings. Serve from crock. *Makes 4 servings.*

❦

SALT COD À LA PROVENÇALE

Allow time for soaking the cod before beginning to cook this dish.

1 pound salt cod
8 whole scallions, finely
  chopped
4 cloves garlic, minced
2 large onions, finely
  chopped
12 sorrel (or spinach) leaves,
  chopped
1 bunch parsley, chopped

1 teapsoon marjoram
Freshly ground pepper
1 teaspoon lemon juice
  (optional)
2 tablespoons butter
2 tablespoons olive oil
¼ cup bread crumbs
Butter

Soak cod in cold water in refrigerator at least 12 hours, changing water every 8 hours. Drain, rinse and place in pan with fresh water to cover. Slowly bring to boil over medium heat. Remove at once from heat. Drain, cool and remove bones. Separate into coarse flakes. Mix scallions, garlic, onions, sorrel, parsley, marjoram and pepper. (Add lemon juice, if spinach is used.) Sauté vegetables in butter and olive oil in skillet, until nearly cooked. Spread half the vegetables in a 5-cup soufflé dish set over spread-out sling (see p. 4). Sprinkle with half the bread crumbs. Arrange the fish over this. Season with pepper. Cover with remaining vegetables and bread crumbs, dot with butter and set in crock. Cover and bake 2½ hours on High. *Makes 4 servings.*

Thirteen

·❦·

PASTAS AND GRAINS

EASY MACARONI AND CHEESE

2 cups (8 ounces) elbow
macaroni
¼ cup butter or margarine
1 teaspoon onion powder
(optional)
¼ teaspoon salt

Pinch of freshly ground
pepper
1 8-ounce package proc-
essed cheese, sliced
½ cup evaporated milk or
buttermilk

Cook macaroni in boiling water for 4 minutes; drain. Return
to pot and toss with margarine, onion powder, salt and
pepper. Make 2 layers each macaroni and cheese in crock.
Pour milk over all. Cover and bake 3 hours on Low or 1¼–
1½ hours on High, or until hot. Serve from crock. *Makes 6
crusty servings.*

CHILI MACARONI

2 cups large elbow
macaroni
2 tablespoons oil
1 15-ounce can chili with
beans

4 whole scallions, chopped
1 15-ounce can chili without
beans
1 cup shredded mild cheese

Cook macaroni in boiling water for 4 minutes; drain. Toss
with oil. In oiled crock, make the following layers: chili with
beans, half the scallions, macaroni, chili without beans, remaining scallions, cheese. Cover* and cook 4 hours on Low or
2 hours on High. Serve from crock. *Makes 4–6 servings.*

❦

MACARONI AND CHEESE PUDDING

16 ounces large elbow
   macaroni
¼ cup oil
½ cup seasoned bread
   crumbs
2 cups buttermilk
2 onions, finely chopped
½ green pepper, finely
   chopped
1 clove garlic, minced
Small bunch parsley, finely
   chopped

3 eggs
3 cups shredded (12 ounces)
   sharp cheddar cheese
¾ cup grated Parmesan
   cheese
¼ cup melted butter or
   margarine
1 teaspoon paprika
½ teaspoon basil
¼ teaspoon freshly ground
   pepper

Cook macaroni in boiling water for 4 minutes; drain. Toss
with 1 tablespoon oil. Stir bread crumbs into buttermilk. Sauté
onions, green pepper, garlic and parsley in 3 tablespoons oil
until softened. Beat eggs and stir in 1½ cups cheddar cheese.
Mix all ingredients except remaining cheddar together. Butter
crock and add mixture. Top with remaining cheddar. Cover
and bake about 2½ hours on High, or until set. *Makes 6–8
servings.*

MACARONI AND BEANS, GARDENER'S STYLE

2 cups large elbow macaroni
   or similar pasta
¼ cup oil
1 green pepper, finely
   chopped
1 large carrot, finely
   chopped
1 large onion, finely
   chopped
1 large clove garlic, minced
1 stalk celery with leaves,
   finely chopped

Small bunch parsley,
   chopped
½ bay leaf, crumbled
1 15-ounce jar marinara or
   thick tomato sauce
Splash of red wine
   (optional)
2 16-ounce cans (or 3 cups)
   large white beans
½ cup grated Parmesan
   cheese

Cook pasta in boiling water for 4 minutes; drain. Toss with 1 tablespoon oil. Lightly brown green pepper, carrot, onion, garlic and celery in 3 tablespoons oil. Mix in parsley, crumbled bay leaf, sauce and wine. In crock make a layer each of sauce, pasta, sauce, beans and Parmesan, repeating once and ending with sauce and Parmesan. Cover* and cook about 3 hours on Low or about 1½ hours on High. Serve from crock. *Makes 6 servings.*

— 🌷 —

LASAGNE WITH EGGPLANT

1½ pounds eggplant,
  unpeeled, sliced thin
½ cup oil
6 ounces (6 strips) lasagne
  noodles
3 carrots, finely chopped
2 large stalks celery, finely
  chopped
1 large onion, finely chopped
3 cloves garlic, minced
Small bunch parsley, finely
  chopped

4 ounces fresh mushrooms,
  thinly sliced
1 21-ounce jar Italian tomato
  sauce
1 teaspoon basil
½ teaspoon salt
Freshly ground pepper
Dry red wine or more
  tomato sauce to make 4
  cups
1 pound mozzarella cheese,
  sliced thin

Brush eggplant with oil on both sides, using only ¼ cup. Brown under broiler on both sides. Cut slices in half. Cook lasagne noodles in boiling water for 5 to 6 minutes, or until limp but still uncooked; drain and pat dry. Cut strips in half to fit crock; keep covered. Brown carrots, celery, onion and garlic in 3 to 4 tablespoons oil. Add parsley and mushrooms and sauté another 1 to 2 minutes; remove from heat. Stir in sauce, basil, salt and pepper. Turn into measuring pitcher and add red wine or more sauce if necessary to make 4 cups. In oiled crock make a layer each of ½ cup sauce, 6 or 7 pieces eggplant, mozzarella and 2 strips lasagne noodles, repeating 5 times and finishing with sauce and cheese. Cover* and bake 1½ hours on High. Serve from crock. *Makes 8 servings.*

For a heartier dish, add ½ to 1 pound cooked meat to sauce.

— 🌷 —

A PERFECT NOODLE KUGEL

Poppy seeds, raisins, sautéed onions, sautéed cabbage or toasted almonds are all traditional additions to this basic recipe.

1 16-ounce package broad
   egg noodles, or other
   shape
6 ounces butter or margarine
8 ounces cream cheese
2 cups sour cream

4 eggs
1½ teaspoons salt
Pinch of nutmeg
Freshly ground pepper
Chopped parsley
Paprika

Drop noodles in boiling water, cook 3 minutes, drain and rinse with cold water. Blend 4 ounces softened butter with softened cream cheese and add sour cream, eggs, salt, nutmeg and pepper. Mix thoroughly into noodles. Turn into well-buttered crock. Melt 2 ounces butter and drizzle over top. Cover* and bake 3 hours on High. Turn out onto serving dish and garnish with parsley and paprika. Serve in wedges. *Makes 12 servings.*

This recipe may be multiplied or divided. The crock will hold 1½ times recipe.

❦

GREEN CHEESE CANNELLONI CASSEROLE

16 ounces ricotta cheese
8 ounces softened cream
   cheese
1 egg
1 10-ounce package frozen
   chopped spinach
Large bunch parsley,
   chopped
1 whole scallion, chopped
3 tablespoons grated
   Parmesan cheese

¼ teaspoon oregano
¼ teaspoon marjoram
Pinch of nutmeg
Pinch of freshly ground
   pepper
1 6-ounce can white sauce
10 crêpes (see below)
1 16-ounce jar marinara
   sauce

Combine cheeses and egg in blender or food processor. Heat spinach in skillet until thawed; turn into colander and squeeze dry. Put cheeses in skillet off heat, and add 1 table-spoon Parmesan cheese, oregano, marjoram, nutmeg, pepper and white sauce. Oil 5-cup soufflé dish. Set over spread-out sling (see p. 4). Using ¼ cup mixture for each layer, alternate filling and crêpes in dish, beginning and ending with filling. Sprinkle 2 tablespoons Parmesan over top. Set in crock, cover and bake about 2½ hours on High, or until cooked. Serve from dish, passing heated marinara sauce on the side. *Makes 8 servings.*

❧

CRÊPES

1 egg
½ cup milk (low-fat is fine)
½ tablespoon oil

About ¼ cup all-purpose
flour
Water, optional

Beat egg, milk and oil in bowl, food processor or blender until combined. Add flour and continue beating just until smooth. Batter must be consistency of heavy cream; beat in a little water if too thick or a little flour if too thin.* Set a fairly heavy 6- or 7-inch skillet over next-to-highest heat. When hot, brush very lightly with oil. Ladle a generous table-spoon of batter into skillet, immediately swirling pan so batter completely covers bottom in a paper-thin sheet. If too much batter has been added, pour excess back into bowl; crêpe will stay in pan. After about 20 seconds, crêpe will be golden around edges. Slip free with spatula, turn over and bake about 10 seconds on other side. Turn out onto plate and continue with remaining batter while skillet is still hot. (As skillet heats up and is seasoned with baking, oil will be neces-sary only every few crêpes.)

Recipe may be increased as much as desired. Cover and refrigerate up to 2 days, then whisk to blend before baking. Or interleave cooled crêpes with squares of foil or freezer paper, wrap air-tight and freeze until needed. *Makes 11–12 7-inch crêpes.*

❦

TORTILLA, BEAN AND CHEESE CASSEROLE

Cornmeal and beans, boosted with cheese, make a dish as nourishing as steak.

6 corn tortillas
1 16-ounce can refried beans
2 tablespoons oil
1 16-ounce can tomatoes, drained and chopped
4 whole scallions, chopped
2 cloves garlic, minced
½ cup chopped mild green chilies or to taste, drained

1 teaspoon oregano
½ teaspoon salt
4 cups (1 pound) shredded mild cheese, not process
1 6-ounce can pitted black olives, drained

Cut tortillas in ⅓-inch-wide strips, resembling noodles. Soften refried beans in oil in skillet over moderate heat. Mix tomatoes with scallions and garlic. Mix chilies with oregano and salt. Divide cheese in 5 parts, other ingredients in 4 parts. In oiled crock make a layer each of tortilla strips (dropped in like noodles), chopped vegetables, cheese, olives, and refried beans, repeating 3 times. Top with remaining cheese. Cover* and cook 3 to 4 hours on Low or 1½ to 2 hours on High. *Makes 8 servings.*

For CHILAQUILES DE CREMA, substitute 2 cups shredded cooked chicken, turkey, beef or pork for the tomatoes and olives, and 1¾ cups "Sour Cream for the Crock" (p. 17) for the refried beans.

❦

STEAMED RICE

Steaming fluffy rice is one of the crock's best achievements. Do not steam less than 1½ cups of rice in crock, or more than 3½ cups white rice, 2½ cups brown rice.

WHITE RICE

1 part converted rice
2 parts water
1 teaspoon salt per cup of rice

1 teaspoon lemon juice per cup of rice (optional)

BROWN RICE

1 part brown rice
3 parts water

1 teaspoon salt per cup of rice

Place all ingredients in crock. Stir to level rice. Cover and steam 1¼ hours on High for white rice, 2 hours for brown rice. At once turn to Low. Rice will keep fluffy up to 2 hours more. *Allow 4 servings per cup of uncooked rice.*

❦

A SIMPLE RISOTTO

This is not a true risotto because it is baked rather than simmered, but it tastes just as good. Substitute 1 cup of any cooked meat, fowl or fish for the squash, if you wish.

½ onion, chopped fine
¼ cup olive oil
1 cup uncooked Italian Arborio or converted rice
¼ cup butter or margarine
8 ounces fresh mushrooms, quartered
2 medium-sized yellow crookneck squash, chopped fine
2 tomatoes, peeled and chopped

1 cup frozen peas
1½ teaspoons salt
Freshly ground pepper
½ teaspoon marjoram
1 10¾-ounce can chicken broth
½ cup dry vermouth (optional; or use 14 ounces broth)
Grated Parmesan cheese

Sauté onion in 2 tablespoons oil until softened. Add rice and 2 tablespoons margarine and sauté until clear. Add mushrooms and sauté until buttered. Mix in squash and tomatoes, then add peas, salt, pepper and marjoram and turn into crock. Heat broth and vermouth and pour over crock contents. Shake to distribute. Cover and bake 1¾ hours on High. Do not overcook. Serve from crock, generously sprinkled with Parmesan cheese. *Makes 4–5 servings.*

❦

THREE-COLORED HAT

Juices from vegetables moisten steaming rice. Good hot or cold.

6 medium tomatoes, halved
and then thinly sliced
¼ cup olive oil
1 teaspoon salt
Freshly ground pepper
1 pound spinach, stems
included, finely chopped
3 whole large scallions,
finely chopped

2 cloves garlic, minced
1½ tablespoons lemon juice
¼ teaspoon basil
⅛ teaspoon nutmeg
1¼ cups uncooked con-
verted rice
Pinch of saffron (optional)
Grated Parmesan cheese
(optional)

Toss tomatoes with 2 tablespoons oil and a little salt and pepper. Mix spinach, scallions and garlic together and toss with lemon juice, basil, nutmeg, salt and pepper. Toss rice with 2 tablespoons oil, ½ teaspoon salt, a bit of pepper and the saffron. In oiled crock, make a layer each of rice, spinach and tomatoes. Cover and cook 2 hours on High. Dust with Parmesan cheese if not using saffron. Serve from crock, spooning down to get all 3 layers. *Makes 4–5 servings.*

❧

ISRAELI BARLEY SUPPER

Israelis, I am told, can make eggplant taste like anything from meat to fowl to caviar. Here it tastes like meat. Begin this dish the night before you plan to serve it.

1 *medium-sized eggplant*	1 *cup pearl barley*
1 *medium-sized green pepper*	2 *ounces pimiento strips*
2 *onions, chopped*	1 *packet onion-mushroom soup mix*
3 *tablespoons oil*	3 *cups boiling water*
3 *carrots, finely chopped*	1 *tablespoon vinegar*
1 *stalk celery with leaves, finely chopped*	1 *teaspoon salt or to taste*
2 *tablespoons butter or margarine*	*Freshly ground pepper*
	Grated Parmesan cheese

The night before, put whole eggplant and green pepper in crock. Set on Low, cover and cook overnight or until nearly tender. Next day, peel eggplant and chop it with seeded green pepper; reserve. Brown onions in large skillet in oil. Add carrots and celery with margarine to onions and sauté 2 or 3 minutes. Add barley and sauté 2 to 3 minutes more, or until lightly browned. Stir in pimientos and soup mix. Turn into crock. Lightly mix in eggplant and green pepper. Rinse out skillet with 3 cups of boiling water, then stir into crock. Add vinegar, salt and pepper. Cover and cook about 6 hours on Low, or until tender. Stir gently. Serve from crock. Sprinkle with Parmesan cheese. *Makes 4–6 servings.*

Fourteen

❧

FRESH VEGETABLES

COOKING FRESH VEGETABLES IN THE CROCK

Vegetable	Shape	Hours on High
Asparagus ·	Stalks	· 1¼
Beans, dried ·	Whole beans, soaked	· 5–7
	Whole or split peas, soaked	· 2–3
Beans, green ·	French cut	· 1¼
	Whole	· 1¾
Beets ·	Shredded	· 1¼
Broccoli ·	Flowerets, matchsticks	· 1
Brussels sprouts ·	Heads	· 1½
Cabbage ·	Finely shredded	· 2
Carrots ·	Shredded	· 1
	Thinly sliced	· 2
Cauliflower ·	Flowerets	· 2
Celery ·	Thinly sliced	· 2
Chestnuts ·	Unshelled	· 2
Corn on cob ·	Whole in husks	· 1 hour 20 minutes
Eggplant ·	½-inch slices	· 2
Green pepper ·	Quarters, strips	· 1½
Okra ·	Whole	· 1
Onions ·	¼-inch slices	· 4¾ on Low, then 1½ on High
	Whole boiling	· 4
Peas ·	Fresh; frozen	· 1¼; 1
Potatoes ·	Thinly sliced	· 3
	2-inch whole	· 3¼
Yams, sweets ·	Maximum 2-inch wide	· 2¾
Spinach, greens ·	Salad-size torn leaves	· 25 minutes tough leaves more

Vegetable	Shape	Hours on High
Squash, summer •	¼-inch slices	• 1¼
	Whole small	• 2 hours 40 minutes
Squash, winter • pumpkin	Any size or whole	• 2½
Tomatoes •	Any shape or small whole	• 1¾

If cooking a full crock, larger shapes of vegetables in center and near top will be less cooked than pieces at sides; allow time for removing tender pieces and letting others finish cooking.

Flavor and texture are always superior when vegetables are cooked on High. Low simply hasn't the heat needed to capture the vegetable's essence.

VEGETABLES NOT TO COOK IN THE CROCK

These are best prepared by conventional methods:
artichokes never really cook tender;
broccoli has good flavor, but color is dull;
celery takes forever and color is unappealing;
green beans are tasty, but turn an unappetizing gray-green;
mushrooms are never as good as when quickly sautéed;
parsnips are best simply simmered;
peas are fine in mixed dishes but not on their own;
turnips are best simmered, then whipped with potatoes.

ASPARAGUS

Excellent asparagus flavor and tender-crisp texture, but the bright green color goes.

Snap *asparagus stalks* at breaking point, stand in crock, drizzle with *olive oil,* sprinkle with *lemon juice* and season with *salt* and *pepper.* Cover, cook 1¼ hours on High. Sieve *hard-cooked egg* over asparagus in serving plate. *Allow 3 servings per pound.*

— ❧ —

DRIED BEANS

Soak dried beans 12 to 24 hours in cold water to cover by 2 inches. (The boil-2-minutes-soak-1-hour method seems not to work as well with beans in the crock as in the saucepan.) Cook on High; old beans cooked on Low can take days to cook tender! Allow 5 to 7 hours for soybeans, garbanzos and other large beans; 5 or 6 hours for smaller beans. Lentils and split peas require 2 to 3 hours; these smaller shapes may also be cooked on Low, about 5½ hours.

If dried beans are to be cooked further in a composite dish, subtract those hours from the first cooking. Rinse them thoroughly, salt lightly and use soaking water for cooking. No alterations of conventional recipes need be made. *Allow 5 servings per pound.*

— ❧ —

LENTILS AND RICE

This legume-and-grain combination provides complete protein. It's a good meatless dish for a casual party.

8 ounces (1¼ cups) lentils	1 bay leaf
3 onions, thinly sliced	2 teaspoons salt
½ cup butter or margarine	Freshly ground pepper
1 cup uncooked rice	Chopped scallions
1½-inch piece of fresh	Sliced radishes
ginger root, peeled and	Diced cucumbers
finely chopped or 1½	Yogurt or sour cream
teaspoons ground ginger	

Cover lentils by 2 inches with cold water. Cover and soak overnight. Next day, sauté onions in margarine until limp. Turn into crock, keeping juices in skillet. Drain lentils. Add to skillet and sauté about 6 minutes, stirring frequently. Add rice and sauté 2 minutes more; remove from heat. Add ginger to skillet with bay leaf, salt and pepper. Measure and add enough water to make 4½ cups. Turn into crock. Cover and cook about 5½ hours on Low, or until lentils are tender. Stir and adjust seasonings. Serve garnished with scallions, radishes, cucumbers and a dollop of yogurt. Good with dark bread and salad. *Makes 12–14 servings.*

BEETS

Even tiny beets, cooked whole, take forever in the crock. So for true beet flavor and faster cooking, grate peeled *beets* into long shreds, drizzle with *oil* and *lemon juice*, sprinkle with a little *sugar*, season with *salt* and *pepper*, cover and cook on High for an hour or more. Garnish with *sour cream* and *minced scallions* or *dill. Allow 3 servings per pound.*

BRUSSELS SPROUTS

Brussels sprouts lose color in the crock, but their flavor is superb.

Drizzle *Brussels sprouts* with *olive oil* and *lemon juice* and season with *salt* and *pepper*. Cover and cook 1½ hours on High. Serve with *browned margarine* or *butter. Allow 3–4 servings per pound.*

❧

BELLA'S CABBAGE, NOODLES AND ONIONS

6 ounces (about 3½ cups)
  fine egg noodles
½ cup margarine
1 small (about 1¼ pounds)
  cabbage, shredded
1 onion, finely chopped
6 whole scallions, chopped
  fine

1½ teaspoons salt
1 teaspoon paprika
1 teaspoon caraway seeds
½ tablespoon lemon juice
Freshly ground pepper
½ cup sour cream
Dill

Cook noodles in boiling water 2 minutes; drain, saving water. Mix 1 tablespoon margarine into noodles. Pour reserved water over cabbage in pot. Cover, quickly bring to boil, uncover and boil 1 minute; drain. Lightly brown onion and scallions in 3 tablespoons margarine; remove. Add ¼ cup margarine to skillet. Cook until browned. With skillet over low heat, mix in cabbage, noodles, onions, salt, paprika, caraway seeds, lemon juice and pepper.° Turn into crock, cover and cook 1 hour on High. Stir in sour cream. Serve from crock dusted with dill. Serve dark bread, cottage cheese and carrot sticks, if you wish, for a nice casual dinner. *Makes 6 servings.*

❧

RED RED CABBAGE

1 apple, peeled and grated
1 onion, finely chopped
2 tablespoons butter or
  margarine
1 firm red cabbage, finely
  chopped
½ cup dry red wine

1 cup whole cranberry sauce
2 teaspoons salt
1 tablespoon cornstarch
1 tablespoon vinegar
Freshly ground pepper to
  taste

Lightly brown apple and onion together in margarine; remove from heat. Add cabbage to skillet with wine, cranberry sauce and salt. Turn into crock, cover and cook 2 hours on High. Blend cornstarch and vinegar and stir into crock until thickened. Season with pepper, stir and serve. *Makes 6–8 servings.*

CREAMY CARROT SHREDS

*12 medium-large carrots,
    shredded (about 5 cups)*
1⅓ cups chopped parsley
*½ cup melted butter or
    margarine*
¼ cup brown sugar
½ teaspoon salt

⅛ teaspoon cinnamon
⅛ teaspoon white pepper
2 tablespoons lemon juice
1 tablespoon orange juice
¼ cup heavy cream
1 tablespoon cornstarch

Put carrots in crock and stir in parsley, butter, sugar, salt, cinnamon, pepper, lemon juice and orange juice. Blend well, cover and cook 1 hour on High. Stiffly whip cream. Add a little cooled crock juice to the cornstarch and stir back into carrots. Fold in cream and serve. *Makes 5 servings.*

CAULIFLOWER

Make a bed on bottom of crock with tender cauliflower leaves. Cut *cauliflower head* into 1-inch-wide flowerets, arrange over leaves away from crock walls if possible. Drizzle with *oil* and *lemon juice* and season with *salt* and *pepper*. Cover and cook 2 hours on High. Serve with *browned margarine* or *butter. Allow 3 servings per pound or 6 servings per large head.*

— ❦ —

CHESTNUTS

Slash an X on the flat side of uncooked *chestnuts*. Turn into crock, cover and cook 2 hours on High. Peel off shell and skin. Use as desired; the chestnuts will be moist and tender.

— ❦ —

CORN ON THE COB

Absolutely superb, the finest corn flavor ever.

Use small unhusked *corn cobs*, pull out the silk and arrange teepee style in crock. Cover and cook 1 hour and 20 minutes on High. Serve in the husk and pass the *butter*.

— ❦ —

EGGPLANT AND RICE SUPPER

Prepare this the night before for an informal gathering.

2 onions, finely chopped	*1 teaspoon basil*
2 cloves garlic, minced	*½ teaspoon salt*
½ cup oil	*Freshly ground pepper*
1½ pounds eggplant, peeled	*2¼ cups tomato sauce*
and sliced ½ inch thick	*8 ounces shredded moz-*
1 cup uncooked rice	*zarella cheese*
⅓ cup chopped parsley	*Grated Parmesan cheese*

Preheat broiler. Lightly brown onions and garlic in 3 tablespoons oil. Cut eggplant slices in half, brush with oil on both sides and brown under broiler on both sides. Mix rice into onions and sauté 1 or 2 minutes. Remove from heat and add parsley, basil, salt and pepper. Moisten bottom of crock with sauce. Make a layer each of eggplant, rice, sauce and mozzarella cheese, repeating once. Then layer eggplant, rice, sauce, eggplant and cheese. Cover* and cook 4 hours on Low or 2 hours on High. Serve from crock, dusting each portion with Parmesan cheese. *Makes 6 servings.*

❧

RICE-STUFFED GREEN PEPPERS

A vegetable steamer, a metal coffee measure and a little inventiveness makes it possible to bake stuffed peppers in the crock.

6 green peppers of uniform size
1 large onion, finely chopped
1 clove garlic, minced
2 tablespoons oil
1 14½-ounce can sliced baby tomatoes, drained, or *3 small fresh tomatoes*

2 cups cooked rice or *1 cup cooked rice and 1 cup chopped cooked meat, poultry or tuna*
1 teaspoon basil
1 teaspoon salt or to taste
Freshly ground pepper
Chili sauce or catsup

Make smallest hole possible in green peppers and cut out stem, core and seeds. Cover them with boiling water in a bowl. Lightly brown onion and garlic in oil; remove from heat. Squeeze out juice and chop tomatoes. Stir into skillet with rice, basil, salt and pepper. Drain peppers. Lightly fill them with skillet mixture and moisten tops with chili sauce. Unscrew center holder from top of collapsible vegetable steamer and screw into bottom. Center 1-inch-high metal measure or other small metal object in bottom of crock. Fit in 3 green peppers. Stand steamer on measure and fit remaining peppers on steamer. Cover and bake about 6 hours on Low or about 3 hours on High. *Makes 6 servings.*

❧

SWEET RED PEPPERS

A colorful salad, side dish or garnish.

2 large (1 pound) sweet red peppers seeded, in 1-inch-wide strips
¼ cup olive oil
1 tablespoon lemon juice

3–4 drops liquid smoke (optional)
¼ teaspoon salt
⅛ teaspoon freshly ground pepper

Arrange peppers in crock. Pour olive oil and lemon juice over them. Cover and bake 1½ hours. Remove peppers to flat dish. Add liquid smoke, salt and pepper to crock juices. Stir well and pour over peppers. Serve warm or cool. *Makes 6 servings.*

❧

GRANDMA'S OKRA

2 10-ounce packages frozen okra or 1½ pounds fresh whole okra
2 onions, sliced
3 cloves garlic, chopped
2 tablespoons butter or margarine

½ cup catsup
½ cup tomato juice
Salt
Freshly ground pepper
1 2-ounce jar chopped pimientos, drained

Separate unthawed frozen okra or trim tops off fresh okra. Sauté onions and garlic in margarine until transparent. Mix in okra. Mix catsup and tomato juice and blend into skillet. Turn into crock. Cover* and cook 1 hour on High. Adjust seasonings. Stir in pimientos. Serve from crock hot, cooled or cold. *Makes 8 servings.*

SOUR CREAMED ONIONS

6 medium-large onions,
sliced ¼ inch thick
½ cup melted butter or
margarine
1 tablespoon lemon juice
¼ teaspoon nutmeg

1 teaspoon salt
⅛ teaspoon white pepper
3 tablespoons instant flour
½ cup sour cream
1 tablespoon dill seeds or
fresh dill

Turn onions into crock separating every ring. Mix margarine, lemon juice, nutmeg, salt and pepper. Toss to blend with onions. Cover* and cook 4¾ hours on Low, then 1½ hours on High, stirring occasionally. Stir in flour. Unplug and blend in sour cream and dill seeds, or garnish servings with fresh dill. *Makes 6 servings.*

ROSEMARY NEW POTATOES

2 pounds small new potatoes,
unpeeled
8 cloves garlic, minced
¼ cup olive oil
¼ cup fresh rosemary or 2

tablespoons dried rosemary needles
Freshly ground pepper
Salt

In mixing bowl, toss potatoes with garlic, olive oil, rosemary, pepper and salt. Turn into crock. Cover* and cook 7 hours on Low or about 3¼ hours on High, or until tender. Serve hot, warm, cool or cold. *Makes 4–6 servings.*

— ❦ —

POTATO SLICES WITH CHEESE

These thin potato slices will have a crisp skin around the edges. Use this dish as a base for complete dinners by adding vegetables and meat or poultry.

5 good-sized (2 pounds) baking potatoes, peeled and sliced thin	Salt
	Freshly ground pepper
	Nutmeg
2 cups shredded mild cheese (cheddar, jack, Swiss)	Butter or margarine
	1 cup broth of any sort

In buttered crock, alternate layers of potatoes with cheese, lightly seasoning potatoes with salt, pepper and nutmeg as you go. Finish with cheese, dot with margarine and gently pour broth over all. Cover* and bake 3 hours on High; remove cover and bake 15 minutes more. Serve from crock. *Makes 8 servings.*

— ❦ —

ALSATIAN POTATO SALAD

2⅓ cups chablis or other dry white wine	2 tablespoons sour cream
2 pounds baking potatoes, peeled and sliced ¼ inch thick	2 tablespoons plain yogurt
	2 tablespoons mayonnaise
	2 tablespoons olive oil
1½ teaspoons salt	1 tablespoon vinegar
Freshly ground pepper	1 tablespoon crock juices
1 tablespoon dill seeds	3 hard-cooked eggs
½ bay leaf	2 whole scallions, chopped

Set crock at High. Pour in wine. Cut potato slices into inch-sized pieces. Turn into crock with salt, pepper, dill seeds and bay leaf. Cover and cook 3 hours on High or until tender. Blend sour cream, yogurt, mayonnaise, olive oil, vinegar and juices to make dressing. Adjust seasonings. Drain potatoes and turn into bowl. Gently fold in dressing. Chill, then serve, garnished with crescents of hard-cooked eggs and chopped scallions. *Makes 4–6 servings.*

YAMS AND SWEETS

The yam, with its red skin and orange meat, is a variety of sweet potato, more flavorful and moist than its pale relative.

Place skinny unpeeled *yams*, no more than 2 inches wide, crosswise in crock, cover and cook 2¾ hours on High, or until tender. Serve in the skin with lots of *butter* and a dash of *nutmeg. Allow 1 medium yam per serving.*

QUINTESSENTIAL SPINACH
(AND OTHER GREENS)

Spinach is one of the best vegetables to cook in the crock because it can be captured at a moment which is next to impossible in conventional cooking: leaves tender-crisp, bright green and remarkably flavorful. Try this delicious method with other favorite greens, too.

In the crock, toss *spinach leaves* which have been patted dry after rinsing with a light dressing of *oil, lemon juice, salt* and *freshly ground pepper*—just as for salad. Cover and cook 25 minutes on High, stirring once, or until leaves are hot but not wilted (some edges will have darkened here and there, ignore them). Serve hot or cool, sprinkled, if you like, with toasted sesame seeds or bacon bits. *Allow 3 servings per pound.*

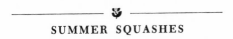

SUMMER SQUASHES

Mix whole untopped and untailed *baby zucchini, patty pan* and *yellow crookneck squashes,* of equal size if possible. Drizzle with *olive oil* and *lemon juice,* and sprinkle lightly with *salt* and *pepper.* Arrange them teepee style to keep from touching the sides. Cover and cook 2 hours and 40 minutes on High. Serve garnished with lots of chopped parsley. *Allow 3 servings per pound.*

ZUCCHINI AND TOMATOES

What this loses in color it gains in flavor and texture.

1 onion, chopped
2 cloves garlic, minced
5 tablespoons olive oil
2½ pounds zucchini, cut in ¼-inch rounds
1 pound fresh tomatoes, cut in thin half-circles

2 teaspoons salt
⅛ teaspoon freshly ground pepper
2 tablespoons lemon juice
Chopped parsley

Sauté onion and garlic in 2 tablespoons oil until limp. Add zucchini with a little more oil to skillet and sauté until zucchini begins to soften. Add tomatoes with salt, pepper and lemon juice and stir to blend.* Turn into crock. Drizzle with 2 tablespoons oil. Cover and cook 1 hour on High, stir gently, cover and cook 15 minutes more. Serve hot, warm, cool or cold, garnished with parsley. *Makes 8 servings.*

❦

ACORN SQUASH STUFFED
WITH AN APPLE

1 red baking apple, cored but unpeeled	Brown sugar
	Nutmeg
1½-pound acorn squash, halved and seeded	Salt
	Freshly ground pepper
Dark raisins	Chopped parsley
Softened butter or margarine	

Trim apple to fit hollow in one squash half, saving trimmings. Fill apple with raisins. Brush insides of squash with margarine. Pat brown sugar into line hollow, then dust with nutmeg. Fit in apple, filling any spaces with apple trimmings. Put squash back together. Cut a notch at each end and tie halves together, fitting string in notch. Tie around middle.° Set in crock. Cover and bake 2½ hours on High, or until squash tests tender. Run a sharp knife through cut, slicing apple in half. Remove string, open up squash and slice each half in half to make filled quarters. Season lightly with salt and pepper, dot with margarine, sprinkle with parsley and serve. *Makes 4 servings.*

❦

PUMPKIN FOR PIE

This will make a pie with exceptionally rich color and flavor.

Cut unpeeled *pumpkin* into 2-inch pieces, scraping off seeds and string. Fit in crock. Cover and cook 2½ hours on High. Remove tender pieces. Return those that are not ready and cook, covered, until tender. Remove shell, purée pumpkin and put in large, heavy skillet. Cook over highest heat, stirring occasionally, until purée holds shape, about 15 minutes. Add ½ teaspoon *salt* and 1 tablespoon *sugar* for each 2 cups purée, continue cooking and stirring until purée begins to caramelize, color deepens considerably and pumpkin is very, very thick; remove from heat. *Use 3 pounds pumpkin for about 2 cups purée.*

For pumpkin pie, make Grandma Rose's Pumpkin Custard (p. 223). Bake in unbaked 9-inch shell at 400° 45 minutes, only until custard is firm halfway between edge and center. Cool and serve with whipped cream or ice cream.

For roasted pumpkin seeds, see p. 40.

❧

ANCHOVIED TOMATOES

1 onion, sliced
2 tablespoons oil
1-ounce can anchovy fillets,
    chopped
Generous cup seasoned bread
    crumbs

¼ cup chopped parsley
6 tomatoes, peeled and cut
    in thirds

Sauté onion in oil until transparent, separating into rings. Mix anchovies, anchovy oil, bread crumbs and parsley. Reserve ½ cup mixture. Oil 5-cup soufflé dish and set over spread-out sling (see p. 4). In dish, make a layer each of tomatoes, onions and bread crumbs, repeating three times. Top with reserve crumbs.* Set in crock, cover and bake 2 hours on High. Serve hot, cool or cold. *Makes 6 servings.*

COOL VEGETABLES, WARM COLORS

16 cloves garlic, minced
6 onions, sliced and then
   halved
½ cup olive oil
3 firm tomatoes, peeled
   and chopped
1 teaspoon sugar
2 teaspoons thyme
2 bay leaves, crumbled
3 green peppers, cut in strips
1 medium eggplant, peeled
   and cut in strips

4 medium zucchini, cut in
   strips
4 ounces fresh okra, sliced
4 ounces fresh mushrooms,
   sliced
1 tablespoon lemon juice
1 teaspoon oregano
1 teaspoon marjoram
1 tablespoon salt
1½ teaspoons freshly ground
   pepper or to taste
1–2 tablespoons vinegar

Lightly brown garlic and onions in ¼ cup oil. Add tomatoes, sugar, thyme and bay leaves and sauté over medium-high heat 10 minutes. Divide ¼ cup oil among 3 skillets. Sauté green peppers, eggplant and zucchini separately until they begin to brown, about 5 to 7 minutes. Add okra and mushrooms to any of the skillets for the last few minutes. Gently mix all the vegetables with lemon juice, oregano, marjoram, salt and pepper. Turn into crock without skillet juices. Cover and cook 2¼ hours on High, stirring once. Cool. Fold in vinegar for a sweet-sour taste. Serve warm, cool or cold. Try it heaped on buttered rough bread, or use as a relish with poultry or meat, or mound on lettuce and garnish with hard-cooked eggs, tiny pickles and black olives. This will keep up to 4 days refrigerated, improving daily. *Makes 10 main-dish to 20 side-dish servings.*

Fifteen

❧

FRUITS

---- ❧ ----

COOKING FRUITS IN THE CROCK

Times are approximate, as they will vary according to season, variety and age of fruit.

Fruit	Time/Setting
Apples ·	HIGH: 3 hours
Bananas ·	LOW: 3 hours
Berries ·	HIGH: ½ hour
Cherries ·	HIGH: ½ hour
Cranberries ·	HIGH: 2 hours
Dried fruits ·	LOW: 4–5 hours
Nectarines ·	HIGH: 1¾ hours
Peaches ·	HIGH: 1¾ hours
Pears ·	HIGH: 3 hours
Plums ·	HIGH: 1¼ hours
Quinces ·	HIGH: 3 hours
Rhubarb ·	HIGH: 2 hours

---- ❧ ----

ROSY APPLESAUCE

2½ pounds tart apples, peeled, cored and cut in 1-inch chunks
1¼ pounds rhubarb, cut in 1-inch lengths

⅓ cup sugar or to taste
2 tablespoons frozen orange juice concentrate
½ teaspoon vanilla

Mix apples and rhubarb in crock, cover and cook about 3 hours on High, or until tender. Cool, mash with fork and blend in sugar, orange juice and vanilla. *Makes 1½ quarts, about 12 servings.*

---------------- ❦ ----------------

JELLIED APPLES (OR QUINCES)

Quinces alone or in combination with apples make an especially fragrant treat.

*2 pounds (about 6) ripe
　pippins or Golden Deli-
　cious apples or quinces
　or 1 pound of each
About 6 tablespoons sugar*

*2 tablespoons brandy
Fresh or candied flowers
Sour cream, plain yogurt,
　custard sauce or whipped
　cream*

Peel fruit and slice in very thin crescents. Lightly oil 5-cup soufflé dish. Set over spread-out sling (see p. 4). Arrange swirl of crescents on bottom of dish, stand crescents on end to line sides and make a scallop border around edge of dish. Sprinkle about ½ tablespoon sugar over these fruits, cover with another layer of crescents arranged to follow contours of dish. Sprinkle ½ tablespoon sugar over each layer, then sprinkle brandy over top. Lay square of kitchen parchment or buttered brown paper on top and press fruit down gently but firmly to make it compact. Set in crock, cover and bake 4½ hours on High, or until all crescents are tender. Cool and refrigerate, covered with paper, at least 5 hours. Unmold onto serving dish. Decorate with fresh or candied flowers, pass something creamy on the side. *Makes 6 servings.*

---------------- ❦ ----------------

JELLY PEARS

*6 firm ripe cooking pears
⅜ cup red currant jelly
⅜ cup orange marmalade*

*¼ teaspoon cinnamon
⅛ teaspoon almond extract
Sour cream or plain yogurt*

Core pears and peel halfway down, leaving any stems intact. Melt jelly and marmalade together, remove from heat and stir in cinnamon and almond extract. Set pears in crock and spoon jelly mixture over tops. Cover and bake 5½–6 hours on Low, or until pears test tender when a skewer is inserted. Use bulb baster to baste pears with jelly once or twice during cooking. Serve warm with sour cream or yogurt, passing crock juices separately in a pitcher. *Makes 6 servings.*

❦

POIRES CARDINAL
(POACHED PEARS IN A RED MANTLE)

Make these a day ahead for best results.

6 firm-ripe cooking pears,
   cored and peeled
⅔ cup sugar
1 cup water
1-inch piece vanilla bean
2 10-ounce packages frozen

raspberries or strawberries
   or 2–3 boxes fresh berries
Sugar to taste
Kirsch to taste
Chopped toasted almonds

Set pears in cold water to prevent discoloration. Dissolve sugar in 1 cup water in saucepan. Add vanilla bean. Arrange drained pears in crock and pour sugar syrup over them. (If syrup doesn't cover pears, make more.) Cover and cook 5½ to 6 hours on Low, or until pears are tender when tested with a skewer. Remove pears and syrup to deep dish. Cover and refrigerate 6 to 24 hours. Make cardinal sauce by puréeing drained frozen or fresh berries. (Strain, if raspberries are used.) Flavor with sugar and kirsch. Cover and chill. To serve, drain pears and arrange in a glass dish. Cover with the sauce and sprinkle with almonds. *Makes 6 servings.*

❧

GEORGENA'S PEACHES

Beautiful use of one of summer's most luscious fruits—try it with nectarines, plums and apricots as well.

6 large peaches　　　　　　　*2 tablespoons light white*
1 tablespoon butter　　　　　　　*wine or brandy*
½ teaspoon mace　　　　　　　*Grated peel of 1 lemon*
1 cup sugar

Plunge peaches in boiling water, remove to cold water and slip off skins. Set whole in crock with remaining ingredients, grating peel over top. Cover and cook 1¾ hours on High. Serve hot with juices. *Makes 6 servings.*

❧

PLATANOS
(MEXICAN BAKED BANANAS)

Fine dessert after a barbecue. Allow one banana per person, multiplying other ingredients proportionately.

1 firm banana　　　　　　　*⅛ teaspoon ground*
1 teaspoon lemon juice　　　　　　*coriander or cinnamon*
2 tablespoons brown sugar

With sharp knife, remove top tip of banana, then slit just through skin along outside curve top to bottom. Gently remove banana by pushing from inner curve. Brush banana all over with lemon juice, then roll in sugar, patting to cover completely. Dust with coriander or cinnamon, slip back in jacket and wrap in square of aluminum foil with doubled-over fold covering open seam. Set in crock, cover and bake 3 hours on Low. Serve foil packet to each guest, banana to be eaten from jacket with a spoon.

PINEAPPLE WITH RUM, MEXICAN STYLE

1 large ripe pineapple   *½ teaspoon nutmeg*
4 tablespoons unsalted   *⅓ cup rum*
   butter   *Sour cream or plain yogurt*
6 tablespoons brown sugar

Peel and core pineapple and cut in 1¼-inch cubes. Spread bottom of crock with 1 tablespoon butter. Make 3 layers of pineapple, remaining butter, brown sugar and nutmeg. Pour rum over all. Cover and cook 3 hours on High, or until fruit tests soft. Serve warm cubes and juice in small dishes dolloped with sour cream. *Makes 6–8 servings.*

SUMMER COMPOTE

Some of these fruits will cook softer than others, but no one will mind; the colors and flavors are exquisite. Only the cherries need be added separately—they have a tendency to toughen if overcooked. Use only fresh fruits; they should be firm but ripe.

2½ cups sugar   *2 handfuls dark red*
2 clingstone peaches   *cherries, stoned*
4 red plums   *Dry red wine*
2 nectarines   *Unsweetened whipped*
1 orange   *cream, sour cream, plain*
2 red or yellow Bartlett   *yogurt or vanilla ice*
   pears   *cream*
1 cinnamon stick

Stir sugar and 1½ cups water together in pot over highest heat until sugar dissolves; bring to boil and boil 7 minutes without stirring or until syrup spins thread. Plunge peaches in boiling water, remove to cold water and slip off skins; halve and pit. Leaving skins on, cut plums and nectarines in half and pit them. Quarter unpeeled orange and flick out seeds. Leave skin on red pears, peel yellow ones; quarter and core. When syrup is ready, add fruits to crock with cinnamon stick in center and pour syrup over them; turn fruits gently to coat each piece. Cover and cook 1 hour on High. Stir in cherries, cover and cook 15 minutes more or until fruits test tender. Turn into glass bowl and cool until warm or room temperature. Add just enough red wine to cut sweetness. Serve with whipped cream or something else creamy. *Makes 6 servings.*

❦

WINTER COMPOTE

Jasmine tea provides an extra dimension to this French compote. Dried fruits are costly, so choose whatever combination is cheapest, but try to get contrasting colors.

1 orange	*½ cup golden raisins*
1 cup dried prunes, pitted	*½ cup currants*
1 cup dried apricots, peaches or nectarines	*1 tablespoon whole cloves*
	½ cup honey or to taste
1 cup dried pears or apples	*3 cups brewed jasmine tea*
1 cup dried light or dark figs	*1 tablespoon lemon juice*
½ cup dark raisins	

Slice unpeeled orange in very thin crescents, removing seeds, and add to crock with remaining ingredients. Stir to mix thoroughly. Cover and cook about 5 hours on Low, or until fruits are tender. Taste for sweetness, adding more honey, if needed. Add more tea, if necessary to cover fruits. Serve warm or cold. Keeps refrigerated almost indefinitely. Good with plain or vanilla-flavored yogurt. *Makes 12 servings.*

For a divine WINTER FOOL, purée some of the compote and fold in an equal amount of whipped cream. Add a touch of vanilla.

❦

LIZZY'S PRUNES

Peel of ½ orange
1 pound dried extra-large
    prunes
3 tablespoons honey

2 tablespoons brown sugar
1 tablespoon lemon juice
2 cinnamon sticks

Add all ingredients to crock with enough water to cover. Stir to mix. Cover and cook about 5 hours on Low, or until tender. Serve warm or cold. Keeps refrigerated almost indefinitely. *Makes 5–6 servings.*

For ALICE'S PRUNES, drain prunes (save syrup to use in place of water in next batch) and set in glass jar or stone crock. Cover with port or Madeira and steep at least 1 week, tightly covered, before serving with sour cream. Keep the jar going if you like, adding prunes and spirits as they are taken. It will keep a very long time in a cool place.

❦

DANISH APPLE PUDDING

2¾ cups applesauce
1 egg
1 egg yolk
2⅛ teaspoons vanilla
Few drops lemon extract
¼ teaspoon mace or nutmeg

14 ounces butter cake,
    sponge cake or lady-
    fingers
½ pint whipping cream
2 tablespoons sugar

Set crock at High 20 minutes before beginning. Blend applesauce, egg, egg yolk, 1⅛ teaspoons vanilla, lemon extract and mace. Trim crusts from cake and slice ½ inch thick. Butter 5-cup soufflé dish, set over spread-out sling (see p. 4). In dish, fit 3 layers of cake alternating with 2 layers of applesauce. Set in crock and lay terry towel over it. Cover and bake 1¾ hours, or until an inserted knife emerges clean.

Lift out and chill pudding, covered. Beat whipping cream stiff with sugar and 1 teaspoon vanilla and pile over dish. *Makes 6 servings.*

For FRENCH APPLE PUDDING, spread cake with thick apricot or raspberry preserves before layering applesauce; spread top layer as well. Serve with custard sauce.

CRANBERRY SAUCE

1 pound fresh cranberries
2 cups sugar
1 cup apple cider or juice

1 tablespoon frozen orange
juice concentrate
Shredded peel of 1 orange

Mix all ingredients in crock, cover and cook 2 hours on High, stirring once or twice. Chill before serving. *Makes about 1 quart* sauce, which will keep refrigerated at least 3 weeks.

Sixteen

❦

DESSERTS

---------------- ❧ ----------------

BAKING DESSERTS IN THE CROCK

Hours on High

Basically eggs and creamy ingredients
(Creams and Custards) · 1¾
Basically cake ingredients
(Flour puddings) · 3
Soufflés · 1

Timing: All of these are wonderfully predictable. Just set the timer and take them out when it rings.

---------------- ❧ ----------------

GILDED CREAM

*½ cup caramel ice-cream
    topping*
Shredded peel of 1 orange
*1 tablespoon Cointreau or
    other orange-flavored
    liqueur*

*1 8-ounce package softened
    cream cheese*
¼ cup sugar
1 teaspoon vanilla
½ teaspoon orange extract
6 eggs
2 cups milk

Set crock at High 10 minutes before beginning. Blend topping, orange peel and Cointreau. Turn into 5-cup soufflé dish and set over spread-out sling (see p. 4). Beat cream cheese and sugar together until smooth, then beat in vanilla and orange extracts. Beat in eggs one at a time. Stir in milk and blend thoroughly. Ladle gently into dish along the sides so as not to disturb caramel. Set into crock. Lay a terry towel over it. Cover and bake 1¾ hours or until only a quarter-size circle in center remains soft. Cool on rack. Turn out onto rimmed serving dish. Cover with a big bowl and refrigerate until serving or up to 12 hours. *Makes 8–10 servings.*

❦

CHEESE DESSERT

3 8-ounce and 1 3-ounce
    packages softened cream
    cheese
⅞ cup sugar
1 teaspoon vanilla
3 eggs

1 box (1 cup) fresh blue-
    berries or any fresh or
    frozen berry
½ cup red currant jelly
1 tablespoon crème de cassis
    or other liqueur

Set crock at High 20 minutes before beginning. Line 5-cup soufflé dish with foil and then with single layer of damp cheesecloth. Set over spread-out sling (see p. 4). Beat cream cheese and sugar together until smooth, then beat in vanilla. Beat in eggs, one at a time. When thoroughly blended, turn into dish. Set into crock and lay terry towel over it. Cover and bake 1¾ hours. Cool on rack for ½ hour, covered with corners of cheesecloth and a sheet of waxed paper. Set in refrigerator 6 to 12 hours. Carefully turn out onto serving dish and remove foil and cheesecloth. Cover top densely with whole berries, stemmed sides down. Melt jelly over low heat and stir in cassis. Spoon over top, glazing berries and cheese completely. Cover with a big bowl and refrigerate 2 more hours before serving or up to 8 hours. *Makes 8–10 servings.*

PINEAPPLE CREAM CAKE

1½ cups (about 23 squares) graham cracker crumbs

⅓ cup (about 1 ounce) finely chopped toasted almonds, walnuts or hazelnuts

3 tablespoons brown sugar

1 teaspoon cinnamon

½ teaspoon vanilla

¼ teaspoon almond extract

½ cup melted margarine or butter

2 eggs

1 14-ounce can condensed milk

Juice and peel of 2 lemons

1 tablespoon cornstarch

1 20-ounce can crushed pineapple in natural juices, drained

Set crock at High 10 minutes before beginning. Set in liner. Blend crumbs, nuts, sugar and cinnamon together. Add vanilla and ⅛ teaspoon almond extract to margarine. Blend with dry ingredients. Reserving ½ cup of mixture, line bottom and sides of 5-cup soufflé dish with remaining crumbs, pressing firm. Set over spread-out sling (see p. 4). Beat eggs lightly, then beat in condensed milk and ⅛ teaspoon almond extract until thoroughly smooth. Blend lemon juice with cornstarch, then mix in lemon peel and pineapple. Stir into creamy mixture. Blend thoroughly and turn into dish. Sprinkle reserved crumbs over all. Set in crock. Lay a terry towel over it. Cover and bake 1¾ hours. Cool on rack, then cover and refrigerate until cold, or up to 12 hours. Serve in wedges from dish. *Makes 8 servings.*

❦

PUMPKIN CHEESE

1 8-ounce package softened
    cream cheese
1 cup sugar
2½ teaspoons cinnamon
1½ teaspoons ginger
¾ teaspoon nutmeg or mace
¼ teaspoon allspice or ground
    cloves

¼ teaspoon salt
1 teaspoon vanilla
3 eggs
1 16-ounce can pumpkin
Sour Cream Topping (see
    below)

Set crock at High 20 minutes before beginning. Butter bottom of 5-cup soufflé dish, then cover with buttered brown paper. Set over spread-out sling (see p. 4). Beat cream cheese and sugar together until smooth. Beat in cinnamon, ginger, nutmeg, allspice, salt and vanilla. Add eggs, one at a time, then add pumpkin. When thoroughly blended, turn into dish. Set into crock and lay a terry towel over it. Cover and bake 1¾ hours or until center is soft but cheese has pulled away from sides. Cool on rack. Cover and refrigerate up to 2 days. Unmold onto serving dish. Cover with a big bowl and refrigerate until ready to serve. Heap Sour Cream Topping over it before serving. *Makes 8–10 servings.*

SOUR CREAM TOPPING

1 cup sour cream
2 tablespoons brown sugar or
    to taste

1 teaspoon vanilla

Beat all ingredients together. Cover and refrigerate up to 12 hours. *Enough for 5 cups of dessert.*

— ❦ —

GRANDMA ROSE'S PUMPKIN CUSTARD

3 eggs
2 cups cooked, puréed
  pumpkin
1¾ cups half-and-half or
  milk
⅓ cup light brown sugar
¼ cup dry sherry

2 tablespoons honey
1½ teaspoons cinnamon
1 teaspoon ginger
¾ teaspoon salt
¼ teaspoon nutmeg
Sherried Whipped Cream
  (see below)

Set crock at High. Beat eggs in bowl. Beat in the following, one at a time: pumpkin, milk, brown sugar, sherry, honey, cinnamon, ginger, salt and nutmeg. When thoroughly blended, pour into buttered 5-cup soufflé dish. Set over spread-out sling (see p. 4) and set in crock. Lay a terry towel over it. Cover and bake 1¾ hours; it will still be soft in center. Cool on rack. Cover and refrigerate for up to 2 days. Serve with Sherried Whipped Cream. *Makes 8–10 servings.*

SHERRIED WHIPPED CREAM

2 cups chilled heavy cream
2–4 tablespoons sugar

¼–½ cup medium-dry
  sherry

Beat cream in chilled bowl. As it begins to thicken, beat in sugar. When stiff, fold in sherry. Cover and refrigerate for up to 2 or 3 hours before serving. *Makes 8–10 generous servings.*

❦

RICH NUT CUSTARD

1 cup dark brown sugar	½ teaspoon cinnamon
1 cup light corn syrup	2 cups coarsely chopped
⅓ cup melted margarine	toasted pecans, walnuts or
3 eggs	almonds
½ cup half-and-half or	Whipped cream or vanilla
undiluted evaporated milk	ice cream
2 tablespoons rum	

Set crock at High. Beat brown sugar, corn syrup, margarine, eggs, half-and-half, rum and cinnamon together until blended. Strain into buttered 5-cup soufflé dish. Set over spread-out sling (see p. 4). Drop nuts into custard; do not stir. Sprinkle lightly with more cinnamon. Set in crock. Lay a terry towel over it. Cover and bake 1¾ hours. Cool on rack. Serve warm or cool with dollops of whipped cream or vanilla ice cream. *Makes 8–10 servings.*

❦

INDIAN PUDDING

This fragile American classic will bake without fail in the crock.

½ cup less 1 tablespoon	1 teaspoon ground ginger
yellow cornmeal	¼ teaspoon mace or nutmeg
1 quart milk	½ teaspoon grated lemon
¼ cup margarine or butter	peel
⅓ cup pure maple syrup	½ teaspoon salt
or light molasses	½ teaspoon vanilla
⅓ cup dark corn syrup	2 eggs
⅓ cup dark brown sugar	Vanilla ice cream
1 teaspoon cinnamon	

Set crock at High. Whisk cornmeal into milk over high heat. Bring to boil, whisking frequently. Turn heat to low, whisk in margarine, syrups, brown sugar, cinnamon, ginger, mace, lemon peel and salt. Simmer gently 5 minutes, stirring frequently. Remove from heat and beat in vanilla and eggs. When blended pour into buttered 5-cup soufflé dish. Set over spread-out sling (see p. 4). Set in crock. Lay a terry towel over it. Cover and bake 1¾ hours on High; it will still be soft in the center. Carefully lift out dish. Serve warm or cool topped with vanilla ice cream. *Makes 6–8 servings.*

※

OLD-FASHIONED TAPIOCA PUDDING

Allow time for soaking the tapioca.

½ cup pearl tapioca	*½ teaspoon vanilla*
1 quart milk	*Pinch of salt*
3 eggs	*2 tablespoons melted butter*
¼ cup sugar	*or margarine*
Finely shredded peel of 1	*Mace or nutmeg*
large lemon	*Whipped cream (optional)*

Mix tapioca and milk in 5-cup soufflé dish. Cover and let soak in refrigerator 6–12 hours. Set dish over spread-out sling (see p. ooo). Set in crock. Cover and cook 1½ hours on High, or until tapioca pearls are translucent. Beat eggs, sugar, lemon peel, vanilla, salt and butter together. Stir into tapioca. Dust with mace. Cover and cook 1 hour more. Center will be soft. Serve warm, cool or cold. Whipped cream is not necessary, but a delicious garnish. *Makes 8 servings.*

RICE PUDDING

5 cups milk
⅓ cup sugar
⅓ cup rice, preferably short-
    grain
Finely shredded peel of 1
    lemon
⅛ teaspoon salt

1 cup raisins
4 eggs
1½ tablespoons vanilla
Cinnamon
Lemon Sauce (p. 227) or
    whipped cream

Set crock at High. Add milk, sugar, rice, lemon peel and salt and stir well. Cover and cook undisturbed 2½ hours. Stir in raisins. Cover and cook 30 minutes more. Pull out plug. In bowl, whisk together eggs, vanilla and a little hot milk from crock, then whisk in most of milk from crock. Gently whisk egg mixture into rice—it will thicken almost at once. *Immediately* turn custard into shallow bowl or it will curdle. Dust top freely with cinnamon, lay sheet of waxed paper directly on top and refrigerate until cool or cold. Serve with hot Lemon Sauce or whipped cream. *Makes 6 servings.*

BEST BREAD PUDDING EVER

If you've hated bread pudding until now, just try this!

½ cup raisins
3 tabespoons brandy
4 large ½-inch-thick slices
    French, Italian or home-
    made-style white bread,
    4–5 days old
Margarine or butter

Cinnamon
3 eggs
½ cup sugar
3 cups milk
1 teaspoon vanilla
Nutmeg
Lemon Sauce (see below)

Set crock at High. Heat oven broiler. Toss raisins in brandy in small bowl. Trim crusts from bread. Butter well on both sides. Set bread on baking sheet and slip beneath broiler until golden on both sides. Sprinkle freely with cinnamon on both sides. Watching carefully, return to broiler until cinnamon toasts on both sides. Cut slices into 1-inch squares. Measure: you'll need 2 heaping cups. Set raisins in turned-off oven to plump. In a bowl, whisk together eggs, sugar, milk and vanilla. Fold in bread squares and soak until they no longer float, about 1 minute. Butter 5-cup soufflé dish and set over spread-out sling (see p. 4). Turn contents of bowl into dish. Sprinkle raisins and brandy over all and mix only slightly so they stay near top. Dust with nutmeg. Set in crock. Lay a terry towel over it. Cover and bake 1¾ hours on High, or until only a 50-cent-sized circle in center remains soft. Slip dish briefly beneath hot broiler to crisp top. Serve warm with hot Lemon Sauce—or plain, if you prefer. *Makes 6–8 servings* (but 3 people have been known to finish it off!).

LEMON SAUCE

1 juicy lemon   *2 tablespoons gin*
¼ cup sugar or to taste

Shred lemon peel into small heavy skillet. Add sugar and ¾ cup water and stir over medium heat until dissolved. When it starts boiling, lower heat and simmer 20 minutes without stirring; remove. Squeeze out lemon juice and strain. Slowly stir into skillet. Add gin and more sugar, if necessary. Serve hot or warm. *Makes 4 servings.*

❦

LEMON CURD PUDDING

The sauce drifts to the bottom and the pudding-cake floats to the top.

¾ cup sugar
2 eggs, separated
3 tablespoons cornstarch
¼ cup lemon juice
1 cup milk
2 tablespoons melted butter
  or margarine

2 tablespoons finely
  shredded lemon peel
Pinch of salt
½ teaspoon vanilla
Nutmeg

Set crock at High 20 minutes before beginning. Reserve 1 tablespoon sugar. Stir together egg yolks, remaining sugar, cornstarch, lemon juice, milk, margarine and lemon peel. Beat egg whites with salt until foamy. Slowly beat in reserved sugar, beating until stiff but not dry. Fold in vanilla. With a mixer on low speed or with a whisk, blend lemon mixture into whites folding together gently but thoroughly. Turn into generously buttered 5-cup soufflé dish. Set over spread-out sling (see p. 4). Set in crock. Lay a terry towel over it. Cover and bake 1¾ hours. Serve at once, spooning down into dish for sauce. Or cool a minute, then turn out onto rimmed dish and serve warm. In either case, dust with nutmeg. *Makes 4–5 servings.*

❦

A CHEWY, NUTTY GRAHAM PUDDING

This is made with graham cracker crumbs, but it seems like chocolate. Although it has no shortening, it is wonderfully moist. Serve it hot for dessert or cold for picnics.

3 eggs, separated
1 teaspoon vanilla
⅞ cup sugar
1 cup very fine graham
  cracker crumbs
1 teaspoon baking powder

Pinch of salt
1 cup chopped walnuts,
  almonds or pecans
Whipped cream or vanilla
  ice cream (optional)
Powdered sugar

Set crock at High 20 minutes before beginning. Beat egg whites until stiff but not dry; set aside. Beat yolks and vanilla, then continue to beat while slowly adding sugar and beating 1 or 2 minutes more. Lightly but thoroughly mix in crumbs, baking powder, salt and nuts. Fold in whites, blending thoroughly. Turn into generously buttered 5-cup soufflé dish. Set over spread-out sling (see p. 4). Set in crock and cover with a terry towel. Cover and bake 3 hours, or until pudding begins to pull from sides. Serve hot or warm, spooned from the dish and topped with whipped cream or vanilla ice cream, if you wish. To serve cold in wedges, line dish before filling with buttered brown paper and turn out after cooling 10 minutes on rack. In either case, dust with powdered sugar just before serving. *Makes 8 or 9 servings.*

❧

MUSCAT CHRISTMAS PUDDING

1¼ packed cups (10 ounces)
  seeded muscat or other
  raisins
1¼ cups warm coffee
⅓ cup softened butter
½ cup sugar
½ cup brown sugar
2 eggs
1 teaspoon shredded orange
  or lemon peel

½ teaspoon salt
1 teaspoon cinnamon
½ teaspoon ground allspice
1 teaspoon baking soda
2 cups flour
1 cup chopped toasted
  walnuts
Kentucky Hard Sauce (see
  below)

Set crock at High. Fit in liner, butter and flour 8-cup capacity baking tin. Steep raisins in coffee in warm place. Cream butter, then slowly add both sugars and beat until fluffy. Add eggs one at a time, beating 1 minute after each. Reserve ⅔ cup liquid from raisins; drain off rest. Mix peel, salt, cinnamon, allspice, soda and flour. Dredge raisins with ⅓ cup mixture; dredge walnuts with ¼ cup. Blend remaining flour mixture into batter alternating with raisin liquid and beginning and ending with flour. Fold in raisins and nuts without overmixing. Turn into tin and cover with lid or terry towel. Set in crock. Cover, bake at least 3 hours, or until pudding has begun to pull from sides. Uncover and cool on rack in tin 10 minutes. Turn out gently onto serving dish if serving at once, or onto rack to cool completely if mellowing. To mellow, wrap in cognac- or brandy-soaked cloth. Wrap in foil and store in a cool place up to 1 month. Reheat in baking tin in crock on High for 1 long hour. Serve with Kentucky Hard Sauce. *Makes 16 servings.*

KENTUCKY HARD SAUCE

3 cups confectioners' sugar   *6 tablespoons bourbon or to*
1 cup softened butter   *taste*

Beat butter and confectioners' sugar together until smooth. Beat in bourbon. Spread in serving dish and chill. Serve over hot pudding. *Makes 16 generous servings.*

SILKY CARAMEL SLICES

A remarkable sweet, super-rich and exotic. No one will ever guess its origins.

1 14-ounce can sweetened   *Chopped almonds*
    condensed milk   *Cinnamon*
Whipped cream

Set unopened can in crock. Cover and cook 4 hours on High. Chill thoroughly. Open can at both ends and slice in 5–10 servings onto plates. Top with unsweetened whipped cream and chopped almonds and dust with cinnamon.

❦

ORANGE SOUFFLE

For a lemon soufflé, substitute a lemon for the orange.

3 eggs, separated
⅛ teaspoon nutmeg
¾ cup sugar
Peel and juice of 1 orange

Pinch of salt
Marmalade Sauce (see
  below)

Set crock at High 20 minutes before beginning. Make a foil collar for 5-cup soufflé dish, as high as room in the crock will allow. Butter and sugar collar and dish. Set over spread-out sling (see p. 4). Beat egg yolks until thick and lemon-colored. Gradually beat in nutmeg and 6 tablespoons sugar. Add orange peel and juice to yolks. Beat whites with salt until foamy, then gradually beat in remaining sugar until stiff but not dry. Fold into orange mixture, then spread in dish. Set in crock, cover and bake 1 hour. Lift out and gently remove collar. Serve at once with Marmalade Sauce. *Makes 4 servings.*

MARMALADE SAUCE

½ cup orange, ginger,
  lemon or lime marmalade

½ cup whipping cream

Melt marmalade over low heat; let cool a bit. Whip cream and fold into marmalade. Serve in bowl. *Makes 4 servings.*

———— ❦ ————

CHOCOLATE ALMOND DREAM

A delightful confection, somewhere between cake, pudding and mousse.

3 ounces unsweetened chocolate
¼ cup butter or margarine
1 8-ounce can almond paste
¼ cup flour
½ cup plus 3 tablespoons sugar
4 eggs, separated

2 teaspoons vanilla
1–2 tablespoons dark rum, brandy or orange liqueur
Pinch of salt
Confectioners' sugar
Candied violets (optional)
Whipped cream (optional)

Set crock at High 30 minutes before beginning. Butter and sugar 5-cup soufflé dish. Set over spread-out sling (see p. 4). In saucepan melt chocolate with margarine; remove from heat. Beat almond paste in mixer until broken up. Slowly beat in chocolate, then flour and ½ cup sugar, beating until thoroughly blended. Beat in egg yolks, vanilla, spirits and salt; set aside. Beat egg whites until stiff, then beat in 3 tablespoons sugar, one at a time. Beat egg whites into chocolate mixture in 4 parts, gently beating until smooth after each. Turn into dish, smooth top and put in crock. Cover and bake 3 hours. Serve in slices either hot or at room temperature but not cold. Dust with confectioners' sugar and decorate with candied violets, if you have them. Top slices with whipped cream, if you wish. *Makes 12–14 servings.*

Seventeen

❧

CAKES, BREADS AND BREAKFAST CEREALS

Cakes and quick breads baked in the crock will be excellent if you
· choose conventional recipes with baking temperatures of 325° or, preferably, less.
· use recipes the total ingredients of which measure no more than 7 cups (count eggs as ¼ cup)—or cut larger ones down.
· order the 8-cup covered baking tin from a crock manufacturer; it makes the best use of space, the locked top makes lifting easy, and there's no need to use terry toweling on top to absorb moisture. But you can use any 8-cup tin that fits.
· make a liner to protect batter from the intense heat of the crock walls: 1) cut and staple together lightweight cardboard to fit the interior snugly—it is not necessary to line the bottom unless the crock has a bottom source of heat; 2) line the inside of the cardboard with a single layer of heavy-duty aluminum foil; 3) inside the foil, staple a layer of brown shopping-bag paper. This liner should be kept and reused. It makes an extraordinary difference in the color and texture of the finished cake or bread.
· don't lift the cover for at least the first 2 hours.

Timing: As a general rule, cakes require 3 hours on High to bake.

Cake mixes: Most packaged cake mixes do not work well in the crock. They have too much sugar in proportion to flour, and the edges brown and harden in the crock. Since they are formulated for higher temperatures and shorter baking times, they are usually too moist on top when they are finished.

Yeast breads: Yeast breads do not work well in the crock.

GOLD CAKE—THE BASIC CROCK CAKE

Two secrets for cake-baking in the crock: use less than 1 cup of sugar for every 2 cups of flour. And use a liner (see p. 5).

2 cups all-purpose flour
¼ teaspoon cream of tartar
¼ teaspoon salt
1 cup softened butter or
  margarine

¾–1 cup sugar
1 teaspoon vanilla
¼ teaspoon mace or nutmeg
6 eggs
Confectioners' sugar

Set crock at High 20 minutes before beginning. Fit in liner. Butter and flour 8-cup-capacity baking tin. Mix flour, cream of tartar and salt; set aside. Cream butter, then add sugar, vanilla and mace. Beat until fluffy. Add eggs, one at a time, beating 1 minute after each. Blend in flour mixture; do not overmix. Spread in tin, and put on lid or lay terry towel over it. Put in crock, cover and bake 3 hours or until cake has begun to pull from sides. Uncover. Let stand in tin on cake rack about 10 minutes, then turn out to cool. Dust with confectioners' sugar, slice and serve. *Makes about 16 servings.*

VICTORIAN SEED CAKE

1 recipe Gold Cake (above)
1 teaspoon orange-flower
  water or rose water

½ teaspoon allspice
1 tablespoon caraway seeds

Follow recipe for Gold Cake, adding orange-flower water with vanilla, and allspice with mace. Stir in caraway seeds after flour has been blended in.

For SAFFRON SEED CAKE, add ¼ teaspoon powdered saffron with other spices above.

WALNUT CAKE

⅔ cup currants
2 tablespoons bourbon
1½ cups plus 1 tablespoon
  all-purpose flour
1 teaspoon baking powder
¼ teaspoon salt
¼ teaspoon mace
Generous pinch of freshly
  ground pepper

⅔ cup softened butter or
  margarine
⅔ cup sugar
3 eggs
2⅔ cups toasted chopped
  walnuts
⅓ cup milk
Bourbon

Set crock at High 20 minutes before beginning. Fit in liner (see p. 5). Butter and flour 8-cup baking tin. Soak currants in bourbon. Mix flour, baking powder, salt, mace and pepper. Cream butter, add sugar and beat until fluffy. Add eggs, one at a time, beating 1 minute after each. Dredge currants and walnuts with ½ cup flour mixture. Blend remaining flour into batter alternately with milk, beginning and ending with flour. Fold in currants and walnuts; do not overmix. Spread in tin. Put on lid or lay terry towel over it. Put in crock, cover and bake 3 hours or until cake has begun to pull from sides. Uncover. Let stand in tin on cake rack about 10 minutes, then turn out to cool. To ripen or to keep, wrap in bourbon-soaked cloth, then wrap in foil and store in a cool place up to 2 weeks. *Makes 16 servings.*

❦

A TRAVELING CAKE

2½ cups whole-wheat
　flour
1½ teaspoons baking soda
½ teaspoon salt
1 teaspoon cinnamon
½ teaspoon mace or nutmeg
½ teaspoon ground carda-
　mom or coriander seeds
1 cup chopped dates or
　raisins

½ cup chopped hazelnuts
　or walnuts
½ cup softened butter or
　margarine
1 cup light-brown sugar
1½ cups thick applesauce
2 eggs
Confectioners' sugar

Set crock at High 20 minutes before beginning. Fit in liner (see p. 5). Butter and flour 8-cup baking tin. Mix flour, baking soda, salt, cinnamon, mace and cardamom. Dredge dates and hazelnuts with ¼ cup of flour mixture. Cream butter, add sugar and beat until fluffy. Add applesauce, then eggs, one at a time, beating 1 minute after each addition. Blend remaining flour into batter. Fold in dates and nuts; do not overmix. Spread in tin. Put on lid or lay terry towel over it. Put in crock, cover and bake 3 hours, or until cake has begun to pull from sides. Uncover. Let stand in tin on cake rack about 10 minutes, then turn out to cool. Dust with confectioners' sugar. *Makes 16 servings.*

CARROT CAKE

1½ cups all-purpose flour
½ cup light-brown sugar
½ cup sugar
1 teaspoon baking soda
¼ teaspoon salt
¾ teaspoon cinnamon
¾ cup chopped walnuts
1 cup finely grated raw
  carrots
¼ cup flaked coconut
¾ cup oil
½ cup crushed canned pineapple in natural juices
2 eggs
1 tablespoon grated orange
  peel
1 teaspoon vanilla
Cream Cheese Icing (below)

Set crock at High 20 minutes before beginning. Fit in liner. Butter and flour 8-cup baking tin. Mix flour, sugars, baking soda, salt and cinnamon. Blend in walnuts, carrots and coconut. Add oil, pineapple, eggs, orange peel and vanilla and beat until thoroughly blended. Spread in tin. Put on lid or lay terry towel over it. Put in crock, cover and bake 3 hours, or until cake has begun to pull from sides. Uncover. Let stand in tin on cake rack about 10 minutes, then turn out to cool. Frost with Cream Cheese Icing. *Makes 16 servings.*

CREAM CHEESE ICING

¼ cup softened butter
4 ounces softened cream
  cheese
½ box confectioners' sugar
¾ teaspoon vanilla
2 teaspoons frozen orange
  juice concentrate

Cream butter, cream cheese and sugar together until smooth. Beat in vanilla and orange juice concentrate. If too soft, add more sugar or refrigerate briefly. Spread over cake.

———————— ❧ ————————

BLUEBERRY CRUMBLES

A cross between a cookie and a cake. Serve it hot, with vanilla ice cream on top, or cold, if you prefer.

1 13-ounce package wild-blueberry muffin mix with canned blueberries	*½ cup chopped walnuts*
	½ cup coconut
	½ cup rolled oats
½ cup sweetened condensed milk	*½ cup melted butter or margarine*

Set crock at High 20 minutes before beginning. Drain blueberries in can. Pat dry, then stir into condensed milk. Blend walnuts, coconut and oats with muffin mix. Pour ¼ cup of butter in 8-cup baking tin. Make a layer each of heaping ½-cup mix and blueberry mixture, repeating layers 5 times and ending with mix. Drizzle remaining margarine over all. Put on lid or lay terry towel over it. Put in crock. (No liner is necessary because crisp edges are desirable here.) Cover and bake 2 hours or until cake has begun to pull from sides. Uncover. Let stand in tin on cake rack about 5 minutes. Turn out onto serving plate. Serve in wedges hot or cooled. *Makes 8–10 servings.*

———————— ❧ ————————

IRISH SODA BREAD

This will almost double in the tin. It is best served warm, with its muffinlike texture; lovely spread with cream cheese and accompanied by a cup of Irish tea.

3 cups all-purpose flour
¼ cup sugar
4 teaspoons baking powder
½ teaspoon baking soda
1 teaspoon salt
¼ teaspoon ground carda-
  mom seeds
Shredded peel of 1 large
  orange

1 cup currants
1½ cups buttermilk
1 egg
3 tablespoons melted butter
  or margarine
Margarine

Set crock at High. Fit in liner. Butter and flour 8-cup baking tin. Mix flour, sugar, baking powder, baking soda, salt,
cardamom, orange peel and currants; set aside. Blend buttermilk, egg and butter together. Blend into flour mixture with
fork. Knead a few times on lightly floured board. Pat into tin
and let stand 20 minutes. Cover with lid or lay terry towel
over it. Put in crock, cover and bake 3 hours or until bread
has begun to pull from sides. Turn out onto cooling rack.
Brush with margarine and brown top beneath broiler. Use a
sharp serrated knife to slice thin. *Makes 16 servings.*

SWEET POPPY SEED BREAD

A most successful tea bread. Use a food processor or mixer
to blend the ingredients. The soufflé dish gives the loaf a
pleasing shape.

1½ cups all-purpose flour
½ teaspoon baking soda
½ teaspoon salt
¼ teaspoon nutmeg
2 eggs

½ cup oil
1 teaspoon vanilla
¾ cup light-brown sugar
½ cup buttermilk
1 2-ounce box poppy seeds

Set crock at High 20 minutes before beginning. Fit in liner.
Butter and flour 5-cup soufflé dish. Set over spread-out sling

(see p. 4). Mix flour, baking soda, salt and nutmeg; set aside. Beat eggs lightly, then beat in oil, vanilla and brown sugar. When thick and smooth, blend in flour mixture. Add buttermilk, then stir in poppy seeds. Turn into dish. Set in crock and lay terry towel over it. Cover and bake 2 hours 50 minutes, or until bread has begun to pull from sides. Turn out onto cooling rack. Serve in wedges either hot, warm or cooled. *Makes 16 servings.*

--- ❦ ---

COOKING CEREALS IN THE CROCK

With a crock, a timer and some whole-grain cereals, you can start an old-fashioned breakfast the night before.

Shape	Liquid	Hours on Low
Rolled oats, any 5-minute large-grained cereal	Milk	3
Cracked wheat	Water	8–9
Wheat berries, steel-cut oats, any large hard grain	Water	10–12

Follow directions on package for proportions of cereal to liquid.

Add a handful of dried fruit or a little sweet spice, if you wish.

Finely milled grains such as farina and corn meal require stirring for a smooth light texture and are therefore not suited to unattended overnight cooking in the crock.

Eighteen

❧

PRESERVES

THE CROCK AS A PRESERVING KETTLE

The crock will prepare superb fruit and juices for making jellies, jams, marmalades and preserves in a kettle on top of the stove. It will also complete the process of making fruit honeys and syrups, puréed sauces, chutneys, conserves, mincemeats and relishes. And simmer succulent fruit peel.

It will not boil jellies and such to the jellying point. It will not reduce fruit butters, leathers, cheeses and pastes—they simply caramelize without thickening. Fruit slices in vinegar and pickles never seem to cook tender.

But what it does do for preserves, the crock does better than anything else.

ENGLISH BITTER JELLY
AND MARMALADE

This master recipe, whether you use plump juicy tangerines, dry lemons or indifferent oranges, makes jelly and marmalade to rival the costliest imports. It is a slow process, but it makes great gifts and special treats and is eminently worth it.

JELLY

4 pounds oranges, tanger-
   ines, lemons or grapefruit
   in any combination
1 large lemon
4 teaspoons ascorbic acid-
   citric acid canning powder

7 cups water
About 2 cups orange juice
6¾ cups (3 pounds) sugar
Scented geranium or other
   sweet leaves (optional)

Shred peel of fruit and lemon very fine. Tie securely in a clean damp cloth. Slice fruit thin; tie seeds loosely but securely in a clean damp cloth. Turn fruit, powder, water, orange juice and bags of seeds and peel into bowl and stir to mix. Cover and set in a cool place (not refrigerator) 24 hours. Squeeze all juice from bag of peel into crock; reserve bag. Turn contents of bowl into crock, including bag of seeds. Cover and cook 3 hours on High. Dampen a large clean cloth and spread over a colander set over a bowl. Turn crock contents into it. When cool enough to handle, securely wrap corners of cloth together to make a bag. Hang bag over bowl to drip overnight. For crystal-clear jelly, do not squeeze; for maximum jelly, squeeze. Measure. Add orange juice strained through damp cloth to make 6 cups, if necessary. Use 1 pound (2¼ cups) sugar for every pint of juice. Pass the juice through a clean damp cloth into a large kettle. Bring to a boil over medium heat. Stir in sugar over *low* heat until dissolved. Then turn up heat and boil rapidly about 20 minutes until candy thermometer registers 220°–221° or when a spoon dipped in the kettle and held horizontally drops the jelly in a sheet. Remove from heat and skim off foam. Have sterilized and still hot eight 8-ounce jars or the equivalent. Set a scented leaf in the bottom of each, if you have some. Pour in jelly to within ¼ inch of top. Cool thoroughly without disturbing. Cover with paraffin or use squares of clean bond paper, tied down. Store in a cool, dry place. *Makes 64 ounces of jelly* (plus a spoonful or two for the cook).

MARMALADE

Seeds, peel and pulp from jelly above	*Orange juice to make 4 cups*
Juice of 1 lemon	*4½ cups (2 pounds) sugar*
	Scented leaves (optional)

Squeeze all juice from bag of seeds into measuring pitcher. Discard bag. Add peel from bag and pulp. Add lemon juice and orange juice. Turn into kettle and bring to boil over medium heat, stirring occasionally. Stir in sugar over *low* heat until dissolved. Then turn up heat and boil rapidly about 15 minutes until candy thermometer reaches 220°–221° or marmalade forms a sheet when dropped from spoon. Stir frequently so fruit won't burn. Continue as for jelly, filling 5½ 8-ounce jars or the equivalent. *Makes about 44 ounces of marmalade.*

❧

SPRINGTIME JELLY AND JAM

Certain fruits are truly complementary: apricots make apples more fragrant, raspberries give plums extra flavor and strawberries lend rhubarb their ripe sweet scent and rosy redness.

JELLY

1 large orange	*7 cups water*
1 large lemon	*2 cups orange juice*
2 pounds rhubarb, cut in	*1 pound ripe strawberries,*
½-inch dice	*hulled and quartered*
4¼ teaspoons ascorbic acid–	*About 11¼ cups (5 pounds)*
citric acid canning powder	*sugar*

Coarsely shred orange and lemon peel, then slice the fruit thin. Follow recipe for English Bitter Jelly (p. 245), using orange, lemon, rhubarb, powder, water and orange juice and steeping, cooking and extracting juice. Add strawberries with juice to crock, cover and cook 1 hour on High. Extract juice again. If there is residue, pass through a second damp cloth. Make jelly (as on p. 246), 5 cups of juice in each batch, using 2¼ cups sugar for each pint of juice. *Makes 13 8-ounce jars.*

JAM

1 recipe Marmalade (p. 246),   every 2 cups peel and
using 2¼ cups sugar for   pulp

Follow recipe as given. *Makes 9 8-ounce jars.*

---------- ❧ ----------

PEACHY HONEY

Drizzle over hot breads as you would a thick syrup. Lovely on grapefruit.

2 large oranges   *About 7 cups sugar*
1 large lemon
3 pounds slightly underripe
    peaches

Drop oranges and lemon in boiling water to cover, cover pot and simmer 20 minutes; remove and cool. Drop peaches in boiling water, remove to cold water and slip off skins. Remove seeds and put all fruit through food chopper or finely chop in food processor. Measure pulp, add equal amount sugar and turn into crock. Stir, cover and cook 3 hours on High, uncover and cook 4 hours more, or until desired consistency. Stir occasionally. Pack, seal and store as in English Bitter Jelly recipe (p. 245). *Makes 8 8-ounce jars.*

---------- ❧ ----------

IDAHO CHERRY CONSERVE

Serve as you would cranberry sauce, with any meat or poultry. Also good heated and poured over ice cream and other mild desserts.

2 pounds firm ripe Bing
   cherries, stoned
1¼ pounds ripe apricots,
   stoned and sliced thin
1 pound underripe nectar-
   ines, stoned and sliced
   thin

2 oranges with peel, seeds
   removed, chopped fine
1 lemon with peel, seeds
   removed, chopped fine
1 cup chopped toasted
   walnuts
5 pounds sugar

Put cherries, apricots, nectarines, oranges and lemon into crock. Stir, cover and cook 2¼ hours on High. Stir after 1½ hours. Put in large bowl. Stir in walnuts and sugar until sugar dissolves. Cover and let stand in a cool place overnight. Next day, stir and put 8 cups of mixture into large kettle. Bring to boil over medium heat, stirring frequently. Boil rapidly 10 minutes, stirring frequently to prevent burning. Reduce heat to low and simmer, stirring, until mixture falls in 3 drops from side of spoon when spoon is dipped in kettle and held horizontally. Remove from heat. Follow directions for packing, sealing and storing under English Bitter Jelly (p. 245). Repeat with remaining mixture. *Makes 13 or 14 8-ounce jars.*

❦

FRESH STRAWBERRY SYRUP

Use as the base for a refreshing drink, adding soda or water and ice. Or pour over pancakes, waffles and light desserts. This syrup can be made with any kind of berries, adjusting only the amount of sugar.

¾ pound ripe straw-
   berries
2⅞ cups sugar

1 tablespoon lemon juice
1 tablespoon frozen orange
   juice concentrate

Quickly rinse berries, then hull them. Add to crock with 2¼ cups sugar, lemon juice and orange juice. Crush berries well and stir. Cover and cook 1½ hours on High. Line a colander with a clean damp cloth. Set over deep pot and pour contents of crock into it. When cool enough to handle, squeeze out all syrup into pot. Add 10 tablespoons sugar and set over low heat. Stir until sugar dissolves, then gently bring just to a boil. Pour into sterilized bottles and seal. Keeps indefinitely in the refrigerator. *Makes 2 pints.*

❧

PUMPKIN CHUTNEY

6 pounds pumpkin, peeled
  and cut in 1-inch squares,
  with seeds removed
1-inch piece fresh ginger
  root, peeled and sliced
  thin, or 1 teaspoon ground
  ginger

1 large orange with peel,
  seeded and chopped
½ cup golden or dark raisins
1½ cups light-brown sugar
1⅔ cups cider vinegar
¼ cup pickling spice

Mix pumpkin, ginger, orange, raisins, brown sugar, vinegar and spice in crock. Cover and cook 3 hours on High, stirring once or twice. Uncover and cook 4 hours more, stirring every hour. Ladle into sterilized jars and seal at once. Process in boiling water bath 5 minutes. *Makes 4 pints.*

For roasted pumpkin seeds, see p. 40.

❦

SUMMER MINCEMEAT
FOR WINTER PIES

1 pound tart green apples,   *2 cups light-brown sugar*
   cored and chopped   *¾ cup coffee*
3 pounds green tomatoes,   *½ teaspoon salt*
   chopped   *2 teaspoons nutmeg*
1 cup muscat or other raisins, *2 teaspoons ground allspice*
   chopped   *1 tablespoon cinnamon*
Peel and juice of 1 lemon   *1 cup sugar (optional)*
Peel and juice of 1 orange   *Brandy (optional)*

Mix apples, tomatoes, raisins, shredded lemon and orange peel, lemon and orange juice, brown sugar, coffee, salt, nutmeg, allspice and cinnamon in crock. Cover and cook 2 hours on High. Uncover and cook 2 to 3 hours more, stirring occasionally. Cool, then taste. Add more sugar and stir in brandy, if you wish. Pack in hot sterilized jars and seal. Process in boiling water bath 25 minutes. Or freeze without processing. *Makes about 2½ quarts*, enough for two 9-inch pies and some tarts.

❦

ZUCCHINI RELISH

1¼ pounds zucchini, very   *2 cups white vinegar*
   finely chopped   *1¼ cups sugar*
1¼ pounds yellow summer   *1 tablespoon cornstarch*
   squash, very finely   *1 teaspoon turmeric*
   chopped   *1 teaspoon celery seed*
2 large stalks celery, very   *4-ounce can diced green*
   finely chopped   *chilies*
1 onion, very finely chopped *¼ teaspoon ground cumin*
1 green pepper, seeded and   *seed*
   very finely chopped   *Pinch of freshly ground*
¼ cup salt   *pepper*

Mix zucchini, yellow squash, celery, onion and green pepper with salt and ice water to cover in bowl. Cover and let stand in cool place overnight. Drain and rinse 4 times. Heat vinegar and sugar to boiling and pour into crock. Add drained vegetables, cornstarch, turmeric, celery seed, chilies, cumin seed and pepper. Cover and cook 2 hours on High, uncover and cook ½ hour more, stirring occasionally. Remove vegetables to hot sterilized jars with slotted spoon. Boil down juices in saucepan until just enough to cover. Pour over vegetables in jars, seal and process in boiling water bath 5 minutes. *Makes about 8 8-ounce jars.*

❧

SPICED ORANGE PEEL

6 *large sweet oranges*
1¾ *cups white vinegar*
2 *cups sugar*
2 *tablespoons whole cloves*

4 *cinnamon sticks*
2 *tablespoons brandy*
  (optional)

Place whole oranges and water to cover in crock. Cover and cook 3 hours on High, or until peel is tender. Leave crock on High. Drop oranges into cold water. When cool, cut in eighths, scooping out pulp. Mix vinegar, sugar, cloves and cinnamon sticks in crock. Drop in orange peel. Cook 1 hour on High, uncovered. Unplug and let stand uncovered 24 hours. Lift peel into hot sterilized jars, adding some cloves and 1 cinnamon stick to each jar. Boil down syrup in saucepan until thickened and just enough to cover. Add brandy, if desired. Pour syrup into jars; seal when cold. Process in boiling water bath 5 minutes. Store 8 weeks before using. *Makes about 4 8-ounce jars.*

※

FRENCH APPLE RINGS

6 lemons, peeled
2 oranges, peeled
2 cups chablis or other dry
 white wine
10 cups sugar
4 pounds firm green cooking

apples, peeled, cored and
 cut in ¼-inch slices
4 cinnamon sticks
2 tablespoons brandy
 (optional)

Put lemon and orange peel in crock. In saucepan, bring wine to boil and pour over peel. Squeeze juice from lemons and oranges and add to crock with sugar. Stir, cover and cook 1¾ hours on High. Leave on High. Strain syrup, discarding peel, and return to crock. Add apple slices, cover and cook about 2¼ hours, or until apples are tender but still firm. Lift rings into hot sterilized jars. Set 1 cinnamon stick in each jar. Boil down syrup to cover rings. Add brandy, if you wish. Pour into jars and seal. Process in boiling water bath 5 minutes. *Makes 4 pints.*

※

DOG AND BADGER CHOP HOUSE SAUCE

For roast or grilled meats.

2 pounds underripe toma-
 toes, finely chopped
2 pounds firm cooking
 pears, cored and finely
 chopped
1 pound figs, finely chopped
4 shallots or whole scallions,
 finely chopped
1¼ cups cider vinegar
½ teaspoon cinnamon
½ teaspoon ground cloves
½ teaspoon ground ginger

1 red chili pod
½ teaspoon nutmeg
1¼ teaspoons salt
¼ teaspoon freshly ground
 pepper
1 cup chopped toasted
 walnuts
3 cups (1 pound) raisins
3¼ cups (1 pound plus 1
 cup) brown sugar

In crock, blend tomatoes, pears, figs, shallots, vinegar, cinnamon, cloves, ginger, chili pod, nutmeg, salt and pepper. Cover and cook 2½ hours on High, stirring occasionally. Purée in blender or food processor with walnuts, raisins and brown sugar. Return to crock and cook uncovered 1 hour, or until thick and flavorful. Pack in sterilized jars. Process in boiling water bath 5 minutes. *Makes about 10 8-ounce jars.*

Index

Acorn Squash Stuffed
with Apple, 204
Advance cooking, 7
Alice Vinegar's Egg
Sauce, 170–71
Almond Chocolate Dream
(dessert), 232
Alsatian Potato Salad,
201–2
altitude cooking, 7
Anchovied Tomatoes, 205
Apple(s):
Acorn Squash Stuffed
with, 204
Jellied, 210
Pudding, Danish, 215–
16
Rings, French, 253
Applesauce:
Country Ribs with,
106–7
Rosy, 209
Arroz con Pollo, 148
Artichoke Hearts:
Casserole with, 58–59
Chicken Breasts and,
143
Tetrazzini with, 154–55
Asparagus, 192

Bacon and Veal Terrine,
121
Bananas, Mexican Baked,
212
Barbados Pepper Pot, 51
Barbecue Sauce, Twenty
Seasonings, 18
Barley:
Soup, 43–44
Supper, Israeli, 187
Basic Boiled Beef, 95
Basic Chicken or Turkey,
Self-basted, 138
Baste, "Spit-roasted," 17
Bean(s):
Black, Pork and, 104
Chili con Carne, 65
Crocked Pork and, 103
Dried, 193
Lima, with Meat in
Stew, 85

Limas and Pork, 103
and Macaroni, Gar-
dener's Style, 179
Navy, in Soup, 42
Refried, Creamy, 36
Tortilla, and Cheese
Casserole, 183
Beef, 79–97
in Beer, Flemish, 87–88
Boiled, Basic, 95
Braised, 80–81
Chili Verde (Mexican
Stew), 83
Cholent (Meat and
Lima Bean Stew), 85
Classic Sauerbraten
(German Pot Roast),
94
cooking in the crock,
79–80
in Cream, 93
Crock-roasted, 93
Daube Provençale
(Stew from Pro-
vence), 86
Deviled Corned Brisket
of Beef, 96
Down-home Corned
Beef, 96–97
Green Pepper Steak, 87
and Kidney Ragout,
125
Mushroom-stuffed
Flank Steak, 89–90
Pot Roast Paprika, 92
Short Ribs and
Potatoes, 91
Soup, Silky, 48
Stew for a Party, 81
Stuffed Birds, 88–89
Tahitian Stew, 84
Thai Sweet and Sour
Ribs, 90
Zrazy (Polish Stew), 82
See also Ground meats
Beer, Flemish Beef in,
87–88
Beets, 194
Borscht, 39–40
Bella's Cabbage, Noodles
and Onions, 195

Best Bread Pudding Ever,
226–27
Beverages, see Hot drinks
Black Beans and Pork,
Mexican, 104
Blueberry Crumbles, 240
Boiled Beef, Basic, 95
Borscht, Beet, 39–40
Borshch from Old Russia,
44
Bouillabaisse, Santa
Monica Bay, 167–69
Braised Beef, 80–81
Braised Slices of Pork
Savoyard, 105
Braised Veal in Osso
Buco Sauce, 113
Breads, 240–42
baking in the crock,
235
Irish Soda, 240–41
Pudding, Best Ever,
226–27
Sweet Poppy Seed,
241–42
Breakfast cereals, 242
Brisket of Beef, Corned:
Deviled, 96
Down-home, 96–97
Broth:
from Bones, 52–53
Lemon, 165
Mexican Meatballs in,
47
Brown Rice, 184
Browning, 5
Brussels Sprouts, 194

Cabbage:
Noodles, and Onions,
Bella's, 195
Quick Hash and, 66
Red Red, 195–96
Rolls, Sweet and Sour,
74–75
Un-stuffed, 69
See also Sauerkraut
Cakes, 235–40
baking in the crock, 235
Blueberry Crumbles,
240

Cakes (*cont.*)
Carrot, 239
Cream Cheese Icing
for, 239
Gold—Basic Crock
Cake, 236
Pineapple Cream, 221
Traveling, 238
Victorian Seed, 236
Walnut, 237
Calves' Liver, Poached,
127–28
Caramel Slices, Silky,
230–31
Carbonnade of Ham, 122
Carrot:
Cake, 239
Shreds, Creamy, 196
Casseroles:
with Artichoke Hearts,
58–59
cooking in the crock,
57
Cross Creek, 59–60
Green Cheese Can-
nelloni, 181–83
Meat and Macaroni,
Creamy, 60
Pre-cooked Chicken,
Turkey and Other
Poultry for, 154
Tortilla, Bean and
Cheese, 183
Venetian Chicken, 145
Cassoulet Manqué, 130–
31
Catalonian Pumpkin
Soup, 40
Cauliflower, 196
Chablis, Rolled Fillets of
Sole with, 163
Charcuterie, 120–23
Carbonnade of Ham,
122
cooking in the crock,
119
Glazed Ham, 122
Knackwurst in Stout,
123
Liver Pâté, 120
Sausages in Wine
Sauce, 123
Veal and Bacon
Terrine, 121
Cheese, 27–32
Cannelloni Casserole,
Green, 181–83
Chili Puff, 29–30
cooking in the crock, 27

Corn Supper Custard,
31
Cream Cheese Icing,
239
Custard Fish Supper,
169–70
Dessert, 220
Dip with Mild Chilies,
Mexican, 35
and Macaroni, Easy,
177
and Macaroni Pudding,
178
and Polenta Pudding,
29
Potato Slices with, 201
Pumpkin (dessert),
221
School-night Supper,
31–32
Soufflé, 30
Strata from the
Pizzeria, 28
Tortilla, and Bean
Casserole, 183
Welsh Rabbit Supper,
27–28
Cherry Conserve, Idaho,
248–49
Chestnuts, 197
Chewy, Nutty Graham
Pudding, 228–29
Chicken, 137–38, 140–
49, 151–57
Arroz con Pollo, 148
Basic, Self-basted, 138
Breasts and Artichokes,
143
Chanteclair, 146
cooking in the crock,
137
Curry for a Crowd,
155–57
Diana, 143–44
Five Flavors, 142
Flemish Fricassee,
152–53
with Fruit, Mexican,
147
Legs with Chutney, 141
Neapolitan, 144
Pre-cooked for Cas-
seroles, Sandwiches
and Other Purposes,
154
Roasted in the Crock,
149
Stock, Triple-strength,
51–52

Tetrazzini with Arti-
choke Hearts, 154–55
Venetian Casserole, 145
Vintner's, 140
Whole Poached, in
Creamy Sauce
(Poulet à la Crème),
151–52
Wings, Orange Curried,
141
See also Ground meats
Chili con Carne, 65
Chili Macaroni, 177
Chili Puff, 29–30
Chili Verde (Mexican
Beef Stew), 83
Chilies, Mild, with Melted
Cheese in Mexican
Dip, 35
Chocolate:
Almond Dream (des-
sert), 232
Calda del Ray (Royal
Spanish Hot Choco-
late), 11
Hot Fudge Sauce, 23
Cholent (Meat and Lima
Bean Stew), 85
Choucroute Garnie, 129–
30
Chowder, Manhattan
Clam, 172
Christmas Muscat Pud-
ding, 229–30
Chutney:
Chicken Legs, 141
Pumpkin, 250
Clam Chowder, Man-
hattan, 172
Classic Sauerbraten
(German Pot Roast),
94
Coffee, Old Gentleman's,
13
Cold Cream Soup from
Normandy, 166
Compote:
Summer, 213–14
Winter, 214
Conserve, Idaho Cherry,
248–49
Cool Greek Fish with
Fresh Mayonnaise,
164–65
Cool Vegetables, Warm
Colors, 206
Corn:
on the Cob, 197
Supper Custard, 31

Corned Beef:
Down-home, 96–97
Deviled, 96
Cowboy's Slosh (sauce),
19
Cranberry Sauce, 216
Cream, Beef in, 93
Cream Cheese Icing, 239
Creamy Carrot Shreds,
196
Creamy Meat and Maca-
roni Casserole, 60
Creamy Refried Beans
(Frijoles Cremosos),
36
Creamy Sauce:
Poached Veal in, 116
Whole Poached
Chicken in, 151–52
Creamy Split Pea Soup,
43
Creamy Tomato Soup,
41–42
Crêpes, 182–83
Crock cooking, 3–7
baking desserts, 219
beef, 79–80
breakfast cereals, 242
cakes and breads, 235
charcuterie, variety
meats, and mixed
meats, 119
cheese and eggs, 27
choosing a crock, 3–4
fish, 161
fruits, 209
ground meats, 57–58
inside equipment, 4–5
making dips, 35
outside equipment, 5
pork, lamb, or veal in,
101–2
poultry and game in,
137–38
as a preserving kettle,
245
reasons for, 3
temperature and time,
6–7
vegetables, 191–92
Crocked Pork and Beans,
103
Crock-roasted Beef, 93
Crock-roasted Lamb,
111–12
Cross Creek Casserole,
59–60
Curried dishes:
Chicken Wings with

Orange Marmalade,
141
Curry for a Crowd,
155–57
Garnishes for, 156–57
Sauce for, 22
Custard:
Cheese Fish Supper,
169–70
Corn Supper, 31
Grandma Rose's Pump-
kin, 223
Greek Meat and
Vegetable, 63
Rich Nut, 224

Danish Apple Pudding,
215–16
Daube Provençale (Beef
Stew from Pro-
vence), 86
Desserts, 219–32
baking in the crock,
219
Best Bread Pudding
Ever, 226–27
Cheese, 220
Chewy, Nutty Graham
Pudding, 228–29
Chocolate Almond
Dream, 232
Gilded Cream, 219–20
Grandma Rose's Pump-
kin Custard, 223
Indian Pudding, 224–
25
Kentucky Hard Sauce,
230
Lemon Curd Pudding,
228
Lemon Sauce for, 227
Marmalade Sauce, 231
Muscat Christmas Pud-
ding, 229–30
Old-fashioned Tapioca
Pudding, 225
Orange Soufflé, 231
Pineapple Cream Cake,
221
Pumpkin Cheese, 222
Rice Pudding, 226
Rich Nut Custard, 224
Sherried Whipped
Cream, 223
Silky Caramel Slices,
230–31
Sour Cream Topping,
222
See also Cakes

Deviled Corned Brisket
of Beef, 96
Dill-poached Lamb
Dinner, 112
Dips, 35–36
Frijoles Cremosos
(Creamy Refried
Beans), 36
making in the crock, 35
Mexican Melted Cheese
and Mild Chilies, 35
Dog and Badger Chop
House Sauce, 253–
54
Double Chocolate Hot
Fudge Sauce, 23
Down-home Corned Beef,
96–97
Dried Beans, 193

Easy Macaroni and
Cheese, 177
Egg(s), 27–32
Cheese Soufflé, 30
Chili Puff, 29–30
cooking in the crock,
27
Corn Supper Custard,
31
Sauce, Alice Vinegar's,
170–71
School-night Supper,
31–32
Strata from the
Pizzeria, 28
Welsh Rabbit Supper,
27–28
Eggplant:
Lasagne with, 180
and Rice Supper, 197–
98
Enchiladas, Layered, 61
English Bitter Jelly and
Marmalade, 245–47

Fish, 161–73
Cheese Custard Supper,
169–70
Cold Cream Soup from
Normandy, 166
cooking in the crock,
161
Cool Greek, 164–65
Fresh Mayonnaise for,
165
Italian Sweet and Sour
Tuna Ragout, 171–
72

Fish (*cont.*)
Lemon Broth, 165
Manhattan Clam
Chowder, 172
Portuguese Stew, 167
Quick Dish, 162
Rolled Fillets of Sole
Chablis, 163
Salmon Mousse, 170–71
Salt Cod à la Pro-
vençale, 173
Santa Monica Bay
Bouillabaisse, 167–
69
Turbot in Onion
Cream, 162–63
Five Flavors Chicken, 142
Flank Steak, Mushroom-
stuffed, 89–90
Flemish Beef in Beer, 87–
88
Flemish "Boiled" Dinner
(Hochepot), 133
Flemish Chicken Fricas-
see, 152–53
French Apple Rings, 253
French Braised Lamb,
110
Fresh Mayonnaise, 165
Fresh Strawberry Syrup,
249–50
Frijoles Cremosos
(Creamy Refried
Beans), 36
Fruits, 209–16
cooking in the crock,
209
Cranberry Sauce, 216
Danish Apple Pudding,
215–16
Georgena's Peaches,
212
Jellied Apples (or
Quinces), 210
Jelly Pears, 210–11
Lizzy's Prunes, 215
Mexican Chicken with,
147
Pineapple with Rum,
Mexican Style, 213
Platanos (Mexican
Baked Bananas), 212
Poires Cardinal
(Poached Pears in
a Red Mantle), 211
Rosy Applesauce, 209
Summer Compote, 213–
14
Winter Compote, 214
See also names of fruit

Fudge and Double Choco-
late Sauce, Hot, 23

Game Birds, 138, 149–50
Garnishes, for Curries,
156–57
Georgena's Peaches, 212
German Pot Roast
(Classic Sauer-
braten), 94
Gilded Cream, 219–20
Glazed Ham, 122
Gold Cake—Basic Crock
Cake, 236
Graham Pudding, Chewy
Nutty, 228–29
Grains, *see* Pastas and
grains
Grandma Rose's Pumpkin
Custard, 223
Grandma's Okra, 199
Grape Leaves, Stuffed,
75–76
Greek Meat and Vege-
table Custard
(Sfogato), 63
Green Cheese Cannelloni
Casserole, 181–83
Green Pepper(s):
Rice-stuffed, 198
Steak, 87
Ground meats, 57–76
Casserole with Arti-
choke Hearts, 58–59
Chili con Carne, 65
cooking in the crock,
57–58
Creamy Meat and
Macaroni Casserole,
60
Cross Creek Casserole,
59–60
Italian Meatballs, 70–
71
Kitchen Garden Meat-
loaf, 67
Lamb Loaf, 70
Layered Enchiladas, 61
Meat and Vegetables
Macedonia, 58
Meatballs Java with
Japanese-style Rice,
73–74
Nippy Meatballs in
Mushroom Sauce, 72
Quick Hash and Cab-
bage, 66
Red Flannel Hash, 65–
66
Rice and Meat, 62

Sfogato (Greek Meat
and Vegetable Cus-
tard), 63
Shepherd's Pie, 64
Stuffed Grape Leaves,
75–76
Sweet and Sour Cab-
bage Rolls, 74–75
Sweet and Sour Meat-
balls, 71
Turkey Loaf with
Zucchini, 68
Un-stuffed Cabbage, 69
Gumbo, 49

Ham:
Carbonnade of, 122
Glazed, 122
See also Ground meats
Hard Sauce, Kentucky,
230
Hash:
and Cabbage, Quick,
66
Red Flannel, 65–66
Hochepot (Flemish
"Boiled" Dinner),
133
Honey, Peachy, 248
Hot drinks, 11–13
Chocolate Calda del
Ray (Royal Spanish
Hot Chocolate), 11
Hot Buttered Rum, 13
Natasha's Tea, 11–12
Old Gentleman's
Coffee, 13
Rajah, 12
Temperance Mull, 12
Hot Fudge Double
Chocolate Sauce, 23

Icing, Cream Cheese, 239
Idaho Cherry Conserve,
248–49
Indian Pudding, 224–25
Irish Soda Bread, 240–41
Irish Stew, Traditional,
107–8
Israeli Barley Supper, 187
Italian Meatballs, 70–71
Italian Oxtail Stew, 124
Italian Sweet and Sour
Tuna Ragout, 171–72

Jam, Springtime, 248
Japanese-style Rice, 73–
74
Jellied Apples (or
Quinces), 210
Jellied Pears, 210–11

Jelly:
  English Bitter, 245–46
  Springtime, 247
juices, draining from
  crock, 6

Kentucky Hard Sauce,
  230
Kidney and Beef Ragout,
  125
Kitchen Garden Meat-
  loaf, 67
kitchen parchment, 5
Knackwurst in Stout, 123
knife, 5
Kugel, Noodle, 180–81

Lamb, 107–12
  cooking in the crock,
    101–2
  Crock-roasted, 111–12
  Dill-poached Dinner,
    112
  French Braised, 110
  Loaf, 70
  Rumanian Stew, 108
  Shanks Caravanserai,
    109
  Shoulder of, 111
  Traditional Irish Stew,
    107–8
  See also Ground meats
Lasagne with Eggplant,
  180
Layered Enchiladas, 61
Leek and Potato Soup, 41
Lemon:
  Broth, 165
  Curd Pudding, 228
  Sauce, 227
Lentil(s):
  and Rice, 193–94
  Soup, 42–43
Lima Beans:
  and Meat Stew, 85
  Pork and, 103
liquid, for crock cook-
  ing, 6
Liver:
  Pâté, 120
  Poached Calves', 127–
    28
  Rolled Breast of Veal
    Stuffed with Pâté,
    115
Lizzy's Prunes, 215

Macaroni:
  and Beans, Gardener's
    Style, 179

and Cheese, Easy, 177
and Cheese Pudding,
  178
Chili, 177
and Meat Casserole,
  Creamy, 60
Manhattan Clam
  Chowder, 172
Marmalade:
  English Bitter, 246–47
  Sauce, 231
Mayonnaise:
  Cool Greek Fish with,
    164–65
  Fresh, 165
measuring pitcher, glass,
  5
Meatballs, 70–73
  cooking in the crock,
    57
  Italian, 70–71
  Java with Japanese-
    style Rice, 73
  Mexican, in Broth, 47
  Nippy, in Mushroom
    Sauce, 72
  Sweet and Sour, 71
Meatloaf:
  cooking in the crock,
    57
  Kitchen Garden, 67
Meats:
  charcuterie, 120–23
  ground, 57–76
  mixed, 129–33
  "Spit-roasted" Baste
    for, 17
  variety, 124–29
  See also names of
    meats
Menudo (Mexican Tripe
  Soup), 50
Mexican Baked Bananas
  (Platanos), 212
Mexican Beef Stew (Chili
  Verde), 83
Mexican Chicken with
  Fruit, 147
Mexican Meatballs in
  Broth, 47
Mexican Melted Cheese
  and Mild Chilies, 35
Mexican Pork and Black
  Beans, 104
Mexican Tripe Soup
  (Menudo), 50
Mincemeat, Summer, for
  Winter Pies, 251
Mixed meats, 129–33

Cassoulet Manqué,
  130–31
Choucroute Garnie,
  129–30
cooking in the crock,
  119
Hochepot (Flemish
  "Boiled" Dinner),
  133
Tamale Pie, 132
Mousse, Salmon, 170–71
Mull, Temperance, 12
Muscat Christmas Pud-
  ding, 229–30
Mushroom:
  Sauce, 21
  Sauce, Nippy Meat-
    balls in, 72
  -stuffed Flank Steak,
    89–90
  Turkey, Savory, 139

Natasha's Tea, 11–12
Navy Bean Soup, 42
Neapolitan Chicken, 144
Neapolitan Tomato Sauce,
  18–19
New Potatoes, Rosemary
  with, 200
Nippy Meatballs in
  Mushroom Sauce, 72
Noodle(s):
  Cabbage, and Onions,
    Bella's, 195
  Kugel, 180–81
Nut Custard, Rich, 224

Okra, Grandma's, 199
Old Gentleman's Coffee,
  13
Old-fashioned Tapioca
  Pudding, 225
Onion(s):
  Cabbage, and Noodles,
    Bella's, 195
  Cream, Turbot in,
    162–63
  Soup, 45
  Sour Cream with, 200
Orange:
  Curried Chicken
    Wings, 141
  Peel, Spiced, 252
  Soufflé, 231
Osso Buco Sauce, Braised
  Veal in, 113
Oxtail Stew, Italian, 124

Pastas and grains, 177–87
  Brown Rice, 184

Pastas and grains (*cont.*)
Chili Macaroni, 177
Crêpes, 182–83
Easy Macaroni and
Cheese, 177
Green Cheese Cannel-
loni Casserole, 181–
83
Israeli Barley Supper,
187
Lasagne with Eggplant,
180
Macaroni and Beans,
Gardener's Style, 179
Macaroni and Cheese
Pudding, 178
Perfect Noodle Kugel,
180–81
Simple Risotto, 185
Steamed Rice, 184
Three-colored Hat
(rice dish), 186
Tortilla, Bean and
Cheese Casserole,
183
White Rice, 184
Pâté:
Liver, 120
-Stuffed Rolled Breast
of Veal, 115
Pea Soup, Creamy, 43
Peach(es):
Georgena's, 212
Honey, 248
Pears:
Jellied, 210–11
Poached in a Red
Mantle, 211
Pepper(s):
Green, Rice-stuffed, 198
Sweet Red, 199
Pepper Pot, Barbados, 51
Pepper Steak, 87
Peppery Pork Chops, 106
Perfect Noodle Kugel,
180–81
Pie:
Pumpkin for, 204–5
Shepherd's, 64
Summer Mincemeat for,
251
Tamale, 132
Pineapple:
Cream Cake, 221
with Rum, Mexican
Style, 213
Platanos (Mexican Baked
Bananas), 212
Poached Calves' Liver
Tivoli, 127–28

Poached Pears in a Red
Mantle (Poires
Cardinal), 211
Poached Veal in Creamy
Sauce, 116
Poires Cardinal (Poached
Pears in a Red
Mantle), 211
Polenta and Cheese Pud-
ding, 29
Polish Beef Stew (Zrazy),
82
Poppy Seed Bread, Sweet,
241–42
Pork, 103–7
Applesauced Country
Ribs, 106–7
and Beans, Crocked,
103
and Black Beans,
Mexican, 104
Braised Slices of,
Savoyard, 105
Chops, Peppery, 106
cooking in the crock,
101–2
and Limas, 103
Roast with Yams, 107
and Sauerkraut Stew,
104–5
See also Ground meats
Porkalt, 126
Portuguese Fish Stew,
167
Pot Roast:
German (Classic Sauer-
braten), 94
Paprika, 92
Potato(es):
and Leek Soup, 41
New, with Rosemary,
200
Salad, Alsatian, 201–2
and Short Ribs, 91
Slices with Cheese, 201
Sweet, 202
Poulet à la Crème (Whole
Poached Chicken in
Creamy Sauce),
151–52
Poultry, *see* Chicken;
Game birds; Turkey
Preserves, 245–54
Dog and Badger Chop
House Sauce, 253–54
English Bitter Jelly and
Marmalade, 245–47
French Apple Rings, 253
Fresh Strawberry
Syrup, 249–50

Idaho Cherry Con-
serve, 248–49
making in the crock,
245
Peachy Honey, 248
Pumpkin Chutney, 250
Spiced Orange Peel,
252
Springtime Jelly and
Jam, 247–48
Summer Mincemeat for
Winter Pies, 251
Zucchini Relish, 251–
52
Prunes, Lizzy's, 215
Pudding:
Bread, Best Ever, 226–
27
Chewy, Nutty Graham,
228–29
Danish Apple, 215–16
Indian, 224–25
Lemon Curd, 228
Macaroni and Cheese,
178
Muscat Christmas, 229–
30
Old-fashioned Tapioca,
225
Polenta and Cheese, 29
Rice, 226
Pumpkin:
Cheese (dessert), 222
Chutney, 250
Custard, Grandma
Rose's, 223
for Pie, 204–5
Soup, Catalonian, 40

Quantities, in crock
cooking, 6
Quick Fish Dish, 162
Quick Hash and Cabbage,
66
Quinces, Jellied, 210
Quintessential Spinach
(and Other Greens),
202–3

Rabbit:
cooking in the crock,
138
Creole Style, 157–58
Ragout:
Beef and Kidney, 125
Tuna, Italian Sweet
and Sour, 171–72
Rajah (hot drink), 12
Red Flannel Hash, 65–66
Red Peppers, Sweet, 199

Red Red Cabbage, 195–96
Refried Beans, Creamy, 36
reheating, in crocks, 7
Relish, Zucchini, 251–52
Rice:
  Brown, 184
  and Eggplant Supper, 197–98
  Japanese-style, 73–74
  Lentils and, 193–94
  and Meat, 62
  Pudding, 226
  Steamed, 184
  -stuffed Green Peppers, 198
  Three-colored Hat, 186
  White, 184
Rich Nut Custard, 224
Risotto, Simple, 185
Roasted Chicken in the Crock, 149
Rock Cornish Game Hens in the Crock, 149–50
Rolled Fillets of Sole Chablis, 163
Rosemary New Potatoes, 200
Rosy Applesauce, 209
Royal Spanish Hot Chocolate (Chocolate Calda del Ray), 11
Rum:
  Hot Buttered, 13
  with Pineapple, Mexican Style, 213
Rumanian Lamb Stew, 108

Salad, Alsatian Potato, 201–2
Salmon Mousse, 170–71
Salt Cod à la Provençale, 173
Sandwiches, Pre-cooked Chicken, Turkey and Other Poultry for, 154
Santa Monica Bay Bouillabaisse, 167–69
Sauces, 17–23
  Cowboy's Slosh, 19
  Cranberry, 216
  Creamy, Poached Veal in, 116
  Creamy, Whole Poached Chicken in, 151–52
  Curry, 22

à la Diable, 129
Dog and Badger Chop House, 253–54
Double Chocolate Hot Fudge, 23
Egg, Alice Vinegar's 170–71
Hard, Kentucky, 230
Lemon, 227
Marmalade, 231
Mushroom, 21
Mushroom, Nippy Meatballs in, 72
Neapolitan Tomato, 18–19
Osso Buco, Braised Veal in, 113
Sloppy Superjoes, 19–20
Sour Cream Substitute, 17
Spaghetti, Big Batch of, 20
"Spit-roasted" Baste for Poultry and Meat, 17
Twenty Seasonings Barbecue, 18
Wine, Sausages in, 123
Sauerbraten, Classic (German Pot Roast), 94
Sauerkraut:
  Choucroute Garnie, 129–30
  and Pork Stew, 104–5
Sausages:
  in Wine Sauce, 123
  See also Ground meats
Savory Mushroom Turkey, 139
School-night Supper, 31–32
seasoning, 5
  tasting for, 6
serving portions, 6
Sfogato (Greek Meat and Vegetable Custard), 63
Shanks of Lamb Caravanserai, 109
Shepherd's Pie, 64
Sherried Whipped Cream, 223
Short Ribs and Potatoes, 91
Shoulder of Lamb, 111
Silky Beef Soup, 48
Silky Caramel Slices, 230–31

Simple Risotto, 185
skillet, heavy, 5
sling, 4
Sloppy Superjoes, 19–20
Soufflé:
  Cheese, 30
  dish, 5-cup, 4
  Orange, 231
Soups, 39–53
  Barbados Pepper Pot, 51
  Barley, 43–44
  Beet Borscht, 39–40
  Borshch from Old Russia, 44
  Broth from Bones, 52–53
  Catalonian Pumpkin, 40
  Cold Cream, from Normandy, 166
  Creamy Split Pea, 43
  Creamy Tomato, 41–42
  Gumbo, 49
  Leek and Potato, 41
  Lemon Broth, 165
  Lentil, 42–43
  Manhattan Clam Chowder, 172
  Menudo (Mexican Tripe), 50
  Mexican Meatballs in Broth, 47
  Navy Bean, 42
  Onion, 45
  Silky Beef, 48
  Triple-strength Chicken Stock, 51–52
  Turkey Creole, 46
  Vegetable, 39
Sour Cream:
  Onions with, 200
  Substitute, 17
  Topping, 222
Spaghetti Sauce, Big Batch of, 20
Spareribs, Applesauced, 106–7
Spiced Orange Peel, 252
Spinach, 202–3
"Spit-roasted" Baste for Poultry and Meat, 17
Split Pea Soup, Creamy, 43
Springtime Jelly and Jam, 247–48
Squash:
  Acorn, Stuffed with Apple, 204
  Summer, 203

Steak:
Flank, Mushroom-
stuffed, 89–90
Green Pepper, 87
Steamed Rice, 184
steamer molds, 4–5
Stews, 81–86
Beef, for a Party, 81
Beef and Kidney
Ragout, 125
Beef from Provence, 86
Italian Sweet and Sour
Tuna Ragout, 171–
72
Meat and Lima Bean,
85
Mexican Beef, 83
Oxtail, Italian, 124
Polish Beef, 82
Pork and Sauerkraut,
104–5
Porkalt, 126
Portuguese Fish, 167
Rumanian Lamb, 108
Tahitian Beef, 84
Traditional Irish, 107–8
Veal Shank, 114
Stock, Triple-strength
Chicken, 51–52
Stout, Knackwurst in, 123
Strata from the Pizzeria,
28
Strawberry Syrup, Fresh,
249–50
Stuffed Beef Birds, 88–89
Stuffed Grape Leaves, 75–
76
Succulent Roast Pork
with Yams, 107
Summer Compote, 213–14
Summer Mincemeat for
Winter Pies, 251
Summer Squashes, 203
Sweet Poppy Seed Bread,
241–42
Sweet Potatoes, 202
Sweet Red Peppers, 199
Sweet and sour dishes:
Beef Ribs, Thai, 90
Cabbage Rolls, 74–75
Meatballs, 71
Tuna Ragout, Italian,
171–72
Sweetbreads, 127
Syrup, Fresh Strawberry,
249–50

Tahitian Beef Stew, 84
Tamale Pie, 132

Tapioca Pudding, Old-
fashioned, 225
Tea, Natasha's 11–12
Temperance Mull, 12
temperature, in crock
cooking, 6–7
Tetrazzini with Artichoke
Hearts, 154–55
Thai Sweet and Sour Beef
Ribs, 90
Three-colored Hat (rice
dish), 186
time, in crock cooking,
6–7
timer, electric, 5
Tomato(es):
Anchovied, 205
Sauce, Neapolitan, 18–
19
Soup, Creamy, 41–42
and Zucchini, 203
Tongue à la Diable, 128–
29
Topping, Sour Cream, 222
Tortilla, Bean and Cheese
Casserole, 183
Traditional Irish Stew,
107–8
Traveling Cake, 238
Tripe Soup, Mexican, 50
Triple-strength Chicken
Stock, 51–52
Tuna Ragout, Italian
Sweet and Sour,
171–72
Turbot in Onion Cream,
162–63
Turkey, 137–39, 153–57
Basic, Self-basted, 138
cooking in the crock,
137
Curry for a Crowd,
155–57
Loaf, with Zucchini, 68
Picnic Rolls, 153
Pre-cooked for Cas-
seroles, Sandwiches
and Other Purposes,
154
Savory Mushroom, 139
Soup Creole, 46
Tetrazzini with Arti-
choke Hearts, 154–
55
See also Ground meats
Twenty Seasonings
Barbecue Sauce, 18

Un-stuffed Cabbage, 69

Variety meats, 124–29
Beef and Kidney
Ragout, 125
cooking in the crock,
119
Italian Oxtail Stew,
124
Poached Calves' Liver
Tivoli, 127–28
Porkalt, 126
Tongue à la Diable,
128–29
Veal, 113–16
and Bacon Terrine, 121
Braised, in Osso Buco
Sauce, 113
cooking in the crock,
101–2
Pâté-stuffed Rolled
Breast of, 115
Poached in Creamy
Sauce, 116
Shank Stew, 114
See also Ground meats
Vegetable(s), 191–206
Acorn Squash Stuffed
with Apple, 204
Alsatian Potato Salad,
201–2
Anchovied Tomatoes,
205
Asparagus, 192
Beets, 194
Bella's Cabbage,
Noodles and Onions,
195
Brussels Sprouts, 194
Cauliflower, 196
Chestnuts, 197
cooking in the crock,
191–92
Cool, 206
Corn on the Cob, 197
Creamy Carrot Shreds,
196
Dried Beans, 193
Eggplant and Rice
Supper, 197–98
Grandma's Okra, 199
Lentils and Rice, 193–
94
and Meat Custard,
Greek, 63
and Meat Macedonia,
58
Potato Slices with
Cheese, 201
Pumpkin for Pie, 204–
5